Powerful Profits from

VIDEO SLOTS

Casino *Magazine's Play Smart and Win*
(Simon & Schuster/Fireside, 1994)

Casino Games Made Easy (Premier, 1999)

Powerful Profits from Blackjack (Kensington, 2003)

Powerful Profits from Slots (Kensington, 2003)

Casino GambleTalk: The Language of Gambling and New Casino Games (Kensington, 2003)

Powerful Profits from Craps (Kensington, 2003)

Powerful Profits from Video Poker (Kensington, 2003)

Powerful Profits: Winning Strategies for Casino Games (Kensington, 2004)

Powerful Profits from Keno (Kensington, 2004)

Powerful Profits from Casino Table Games (Kensington, 2004)

Powerful Profits from Internet Gambling (Kensington, 2005)

Powerful Profits from

VIDEO SLOTS

VICTOR H. ROYER

LYLE STUART
Kensington Publishing Corp.
www.kensingtonbooks.com

LYLE STUART BOOKS are published by

Kensington Publishing Corp.
850 Third Avenue
New York, NY 10022

All Kensington titles, imprints, and distributed lines are available at special quantity discounts for bulk purchases for sales promotions, premiums, fund-raising, educational, or institutional use. Special book excerpts or customized printings can also be created to fit specific needs. For details, write or phone the office of the Kensington special sales manager: Kensington Publishing Corp., 850 Third Avenue, New York, NY 10022, attn: Special Sales Department; phone 1-800-221-2647.

Lyle Stuart is a trademark of Kensington Publishing Corp.

First printing: May 2005

10 9 8 7 6 5 4 3 2 1

Printed in the United States of America

ISBN 0-8184-0644-5

This book is gratefully dedicated to

Ed Rogich

"Veni, vidi, vici"—I came, I saw, I conquered.

—JULIUS CAESAR

Remember this each time you go to a casino.

Contents

Foreword

The future is here. Not so long ago just the mere concept of a "video" slot machine seemed so odd as to be unthinkable. Less than two decades ago, some of the first video slot machines were crude displays that attempted to show the 3-reel slot machine as a video display. I know, because I was one of the first people to play them. These machines were odd looking and clunky, and didn't have any of the appeal and pizzazz of the traditional reel slots. They were almost universally disliked by casino players. The only video slots that had any kind of appeal were the video keno machines, and even they seemed odd and complicated. Oh, how ancient that time now seems, and how far and how fast we have come!

The world of video slots exploded onto the scene in the mid-1990s, and the explosion continues. Thanks to video slots, the casinos of the twenty-first century have a distinctly new feel to them. A new feel, and a new look. Modern casinos don't look anything like those of merely a decade and a half ago. Although the floor plan of the casino may be similar, and the layout more or less traditional, that is where the similarity ends. While some of the older casinos may still enjoy a remnant of the old-time "feel," most of the casinos where we now play were built within the last fifteen years. They are all new, and were built from the ground up around the slot machine. The casino slot floor, and the rest of the floor plans for all the modern casinos, revolve around this one concept—the slot machine. More important in the past five years, around the *video* slot machine.

Even though many slot players and casino visitors do not yet know that all slot machines are computerized, regardless of whether they still look like the old handle-pulling reel spinners, such players can easily recognize a video slot machine. It has a monitor, and on this is displayed a huge variety of possibilities. There are games with 5 lines, 9 lines, 20 lines, 40 lines, and even 100 lines, and more. These are all paylines crisscrossing the screen, and making larger and larger wagers, and bigger and bigger wins, more possible. These machines have such a variety of pay symbols as to make your head spin. The designers of the old-style reel spinners are spinning in disbelief. These new video slot machines are nothing like the old clunkers, those old video displays that tried to mimic the traditional reel spinners. The new video slot machines are sophisticated games that take full advantage of the advances in computer technology. They are the very best of the casino games and the latest in casino gaming. They are most definitely *not* your father's old slot machines; they are the modern toys for the adults who have grown up with video games, first in arcades, then on the computer, later on palm-held games, and now on the Internet. These video slot machines are not only on the cutting edge of computer and gaming technology, but they are also by far the greatest innovations in the future of casino gaming. That future—so far-fetched just a few years ago—is now already all around us. The games you will read about in this book are already being installed on the floor of your favorite casino.

Incredible advances in computer technology have made this possible, not just in the games themselves, but mostly in the hardware—specifically, in the memory capacity of the computer processors that run the systems and the speed of these processors. Also key to the stunningly fast evolution of the video slot machine was the tremendous vision of the game designers themselves and the manufacturers. People like Joe Kaminkow of International Game Technology (IGT) and other brilliant concept designers have made these games possible. It is their vision that has combined the technological advances in computer hardware and software with the appeal of the games to the casino players. Themed games, based on known and culturally identifiable icons, have made these slot machines among the best and most popular games worldwide. Games like *Sinatra*™, *I Love Lucy*®, *The Munsters*™, *Beverly Hillbillies*™, *Addams Family*™, and *Wheel of Fortune*®, just to name a few, have become the most loved games among all the video slots on the modern casino floor. Such a combination of cultural iconism and technological ingenuity is unique in the world of human endeavor. In no other industry is this blend of the uniquely new and the uniquely familiar so well positioned and so well conceived. In these modern video slot machines, the vision of the innovator, the skills of the technician, the goal of the manufacturer, and the pleasure of the consumer have been skillfully and beautifully combined. This new whole, which is much more than the sum of its parts, has come to present us with a uniquely new challenge. We, the casino players of the twenty-first century, now have not only an overwhelming choice of machines and games, but also the great challenge of finding just the right ones with the blend of just the right amount of knowledge and luck to make us winners.

Contrary to popular opinion, it *is* possible to win on a video slot machine. *Especially* on a *video* slot machine. This is due to a combination of factors, as follow:

- A video slot machine offers many more combinations for winning events than traditional single payline reel spinners, and therefore many more opportunities for wins, more frequent wins, and bigger wins.

- A video slot machine offers tiered bonuses, many of which contribute substantially to the overall payback of the machine, making you a certain winner once you enter such bonusing rounds, thereby enabling you to make a winning event pay many times your investment.

- A video slot machine is programmed at a specific payback percentage. That means that it must make these pays over its life cycle, thereby making it possible for you to maximize your wins and minimize your losses if you learn what to look for as key indicators of the better games among the various video slot machines found on the casino floor.

- Contrary to popular belief, a video slot machine that is set to hold, say, 4 percent for the house, is not a money-sucking vacuum, because this also means it has to *pay out* 96 percent of the time, overall. And similarly so for whatever paybacks such machines may have.

- A video slot machine is a sophisticated device that is a gambling game, and as such it is among the class of other gambling games that require knowledge, expertise, and skill to make winning events possible.

Although mathematicians will tell you that something with an in-built program that calls for the machine to always "hold" a set percentage for the house can't be beaten, this doesn't take into account the reality of your very finite exposure to the game. The mathematics that go into these games, and into the calculations of the game's overall payback and hold percentages, are complex. They rely on the theory of probability as vested in a very large sampling, firmly imbedded in the theory of the infinite parity of occurrences. This may be exciting to a math geek, but for your financial success, or failure, when playing your favorite video slot machine this day, in this casino, such theorizing has little importance. While the overall principles behind the mathematical theory may be valid when considering the very long term of the game, the fact remains that for the next hour that you may play it such frequencies will not necessarily display themselves to match the theoretical parity. Nevertheless, it is meaningful to know which machines and games are the better paying ones, as based on their theoretical profile.

This is the crux of the gambler's ongoing dilemma: Is it better to play games that are mathematically beatable, possibly investing a lifetime to validate the theory and in the end make that fraction of the percentage profit—or is it better to know the math and the game's theory but learn to recognize the advantages available in the moment? To the gaming experts who are in the "math only" club, the answer is clear: play only games that can have a mathematically verifiable advantage for the player, over the long term. Of course the words *long term* may mean a whole other thing when viewed from the infinite perspective, rather than merely from a sampling that a human lifetime can accommodate. You see, the major problem with this kind of thinking and this approach to your gambling is that the words *long term* and *mathematical advantage* are relative. They aren't finite. A mathematical advantage is nothing more than a consensus among people who think alike, that something they have agreed to call math exists, and will produce that result. It's kind of like taking an orange and holding it in front of a mirror, then using the reflection in the mirror to validate the theory that this *is* an orange. It's nice and neat, but doesn't do anything for the person who wants to know if the orange can be eaten or how it tastes.

The other concept the math experts fall in love with is

long term. In the laboratory testing of video slots, the game's programs are usually put through about 10 million events. This number is considered to be a statistically sufficient sampling to validate the theory of the frequency of occurrence of the various combinations among the possibilities inherent in the game's program. In some cases, tests of 3 million events are sufficient, while in others, tests of 50 million events may be required. Overall, however, the general consensus among the gaming laboratories that test these programs is about 10 million events. The problem is, of course, that these are artificially imposed limits that we, the humans, put on these series of tests and numbered events, because they seem so large to us, relative to the human life span. To play 10 million events in a casino would take a human being about 55 to 60 years, depending on the game and the player's ability to play it faster, slower, and for how many uninterrupted hours per day. So, in the long term as relative to the human life span, these events may indeed provide the basis for a sound mathematical theory. But—the universe is infinite, as far as we know. So, what about 100 million events, spanning some 500 years of a human player? What about 100,000 years? How about 6 billion years? Those events will continue to occur, if only in conceptual theory, for as many billions of years as there may be in the history of our universe, regardless of whether there actually are any human beings around to count them. And *that* is the true test of the long term.

We could, of course, spend the whole book discussing these subjects, but the simple point here is that even machines that are, theoretically, programmed to hold certain percentages for the house must also equally pay out the largest portion of those percentages programmed for pays. Assuming that we agree with the math behind all of this, the simple truth is that a video slot machine that is set to "hold," say, 4 percent for the house must also by those same programming principles pay out 96 percent of the time. We also know that the reality seldom exactly mirrors the theory, and therefore the real truth is that whenever you will be playing a video slot machine, you will either hit it for pays that are far *more* than the math theory indicates you should get, or get far *fewer* paying events than this same theory also indicates. Therefore, to try to combat the machine for your financial profits in the very short and very finite slice of your overall exposure to that machine and its game program, it would be futile to try and mirror the statistics and play only to validate the theory.

To win money from these machines you have to learn skills that will allow you to select the right machine, play it the correct way, and learn to recognize when you catch it in the right cycle. Machine cycles are perceptual situations that we learn to experience and recognize, and although the programmers who designed the algorithm that actually runs the machine will always deny that anything like it exists, the reality proves otherwise. If you read my book *Powerful Profits from Slots* (March 2003), in chapter 10 you will find the complete answer to this. You will see why machines that are as random as current technology can make them nonetheless have quirks that we can recognize as patterns, and use as "cycles" in our perceptual understanding of the video slot machines, and how to hit them at the right time for a financial profit.

Beating the video slots for financial profits doesn't mean you have to defeat the machine's programming or its payback and withholding percentages. This is perhaps the greatest fallacy of the "math only" club, and the approach that is so forcefully rammed down the throats of gamblers by the zealous proponents of the "mathematically sound" strategies for casino games. While I agree that these are important, it is counterproductive for math experts to go on television and say things like: "Anything that you have heard or read that says you can win on a game that is less than a 100 percent payback game are lies. All those people who tell you this can be done are liars." These statements, made on national television by some of the most prominent "experts" in gambling theory, serve no purpose other than to mislead the public. Fortunately, people in general aren't as stupid as these persons may think they are, and the general gaming world thrives regardless of these misguided and inaccurate statements.

The main difference is in the goals. Math and gambling game theorists know only one small range of parameters upon which they have decided to agree. Therefore, whenever they see an orange, they hold it up to a mirror and if the image shows an orange they say, "Ahhh! See? It is an orange because our tests prove it! And therefore anyone who says it isn't an orange is a liar. Anything you have heard that says this may not be an orange is a lie." That's precisely the kind of narrow thinking that I just mentioned. The problem is that these "experts" are interested only in validating the theory, and as long as they can find plenty of mirrors they'll continue to be happily ignorant of the reality of the world around them.

Of course we all know that the object of gambling is to win money. To do this does not necessarily involve the long term nor invoke the gods of the mathematical theories. The rest of us—the casino players of video slot machines—have far less "noble" and far shorter goals in mind. We want to make a profit and to have fun. We don't much care whether this is called an orange or not, or how it may be proven to be one; we care about whether it can be eaten and how it tastes. Metaphorically, this simply means that we want to know if the game is a good one for our gaming investment, and if it is likely to be profitable. These are our goals, and the infinite be damned.

This fundamental difference between the mathematical theorists of gambling games, and the players' actual experiences with these games, illustrates the conflict between those who only pick something with a tiny edge in accordance with that theory and then spend a lifetime trying to grind out those tiny wins, and those who are interested in having a great time today, on this vacation, and making a big profit *right now*. Grinding it out in the casino is not fun. I know, because I tried it. I prefer to go to a casino, select the best game I can find, based on my knowledge of the games and the casinos, and then give that game my best shot for this day, with my allocated bankroll for this session. This gives me the biggest bang for the buck. If I lose, I lose a portion of my session bankroll. But if I win, I win many thousands of dollars, far and far above what the poor, tired, old grinders will ever achieve playing with the mathematical theories. Just one win like that is enough to overcome a very long and protracted streak of losing events. Winning is not forecast by mathematics and made possible only by the math theory applicable to that game. Winning money is possible for you, the human player, based on your knowledge, skills, and the correct, timely, and skillful *application* of those skills and that knowledge and experience. No laboratory theory can take the place of this, and no theory can take the place of the reality. The reality of the world of gambling and gambling games is one of chaos, not of mathematical order. Predictions are possible only by the human player, because the machine is a machine and only an individual who can think beyond the parameters of the machine's program can find a way to beat it. And that's where the powerful profits from video slots truly come from.

Powerful Profits from

VIDEO SLOTS

Video Slots Overview

I love video slots. Among all the casino games that I find exciting and stimulating, video slots rank very high on my scale. Why? Because, they are interesting and fun to play and because they are among the best paying casino games now available. Playing casino games should always be fun, first and foremost. If it isn't why play? As strange as it may seem, many people go to casinos and play various games—and they don't enjoy it. Perhaps they have expectations far above the reality of what their action can plausibly get them, and therefore they're never happy even when they do win. Anytime you walk out of the casino and you have more money in your pocket, billfold, or purse than when you arrived, that's a good day and certainly a cause for celebration. You won, you beat the games. If you also had fun doing it, so much the better. You *should* have fun winning money, because then you enjoy the process as well as the success. And if you don't happen to win that particular day, or that session, well, there's always tomorrow. As long as you know that you played the best games that you could find, and played them as well as you possibly could—armed with all the knowledge that you have learned—you will also realize that occasional losing sessions will happen. If you realize this, then you will have fun regardless of whether or not this particular casino visit was profitable. You will realize that the next visit can, and possibly will, be profitable, much more so than this one losing visit.

This is the proper and correct mind-set for the successful gambler, and the successful, and happy, casino player. Even if you are only a casual player who only visits a casino infrequently, you will know that having fun at these games and making a profit from your play are not mutually exclusive. There are many experts who are of the opinion that playing casino games for profit requires a daily grind for small percentages, to shave the house edge in your favor as much as possible by the tiny percentages, or fractions of a percentage, that you can accomplish on those few games that will allow such skills to be practiced. While this approach can and does work, professional players rarely have fun doing this. The stresses of the required concentration and skills, and the maintenance of their bankroll and proper wagering sequences, often erode any and all enjoyment from just the pure fact of the fun of playing in the casino. If this is your approach to casino games, there's nothing wrong with it and you can perhaps find a certain amount of pleasure in this method of playing as well, but I think that having fun is one of the key ingredients of a successful player. When you are confident in your skills and abilities, and enjoy the pleasure and personality of the game, you are far more likely to attract Lady Luck to *you*. Yes, this may be unscientific to a point, but just about any psychologist worth his or her degree will tell you that a positive attitude and a positive outlook on life are key ingredients in success, be it in business, personal life, or in anything you may do. Casino gaming is no different.

If you arrive at the casino with a defeatist attitude, convinced that you will lose your money, well, then, guess what? You will lose, and then you will feel validated in your prior opinions. Psychologists would call this the "subconscious syndrome of defeatist reaffirmation," or something to that effect. You see, when you convince yourself that you will be a loser, then you will play in a manner that will reaffirm this. Subconsciously, you will look for ways to lose, because that's what you have convinced yourself should be the outcome of your casino visit, or your play for this game, or session. Even without knowing it, you will not play as well as you could, and when you lose you will therefore have reaffirmed your initial goal, which was to lose. This kind of psychological predisposition toward failure is manifest in many different walks of life, and in many disciplines.

Casino gaming is no different, and your successes and failures are due to "bad luck" only a small portion of the time. Most of the time if you lose, you lose either because you didn't have the knowledge and skills required to make the game pay at its best potential, or you arrived convinced you would lose and subconsciously sought out ways and means to accomplish the loss. There's a whole lot more to succeeding in gambling than just the act of playing the game. You may see a baseball player hit a home run, and it looks effortless, or see a pitcher pitch a no-hitter, and it all seems like clockwork. What you don't see are the 20 years of learning the skills in order to make it look so easy and effortless, nor do you see the mental preparation that each successful baseball player, or athlete, goes through prior to the game precisely and specifically to achieve the positive mental attitude of a winner. Ask any athlete, or any successful person in any business, and they will tell you that mental effort and preparation are 90 percent of the battle, and only 10 percent are the actual physical skills required to do the task.

Gambling is no different, and playing video slots falls smack in the middle of it. Video slots are slot machines, and mathematically they are mostly set to hold money for the house over the long term. It is true that the vast majority of the games in any modern casino are house games, and video slots are among them. Slots are almost always programmed to hold from 1 to 12 percent for the house, and sometimes even more. Mathematically this means that any strategy based solely on mathematics is a defeatist strategy. If you happen to win, you pass it off as blind luck and immediately begin to look for something where you can lose these winnings back in a hurry, because in your subconscious you will never be happy winning on these games because you have come to believe that only mathematically sound player-positive expectation games can make you a winner. You are, therefore, trying to be a machine, forced to try and play like one. That is a prescription for more disaster, because you're not a machine, you're a human being, and trying to deny yourself the abilities of a human being means you are throwing out 90 percent of your winning potential.

It is not necessary for you to think this way, or to approach casino gaming from such limited perspectives. I have personally spoken to the firmware engineers who design the programs for the video slots that I will show you in this book, and they say the same thing: "While the machines are programmed to be random, and to 'hold' and 'pay back' those stated percentages, these are only forecast numbers based on the *most probable* results arrived at after testing the game through about 10 million events. This doesn't mean that the machine will always do so. It may take several years for the game to reach such forecast parity. Most of the time a machine that is set to 'pay back,' say, 94.7 percent, will average a field pay rate of either about 38.7 percent, or about 161.3 percent. Basically, this simply means that sometimes the machine will pay a lot, and at other time almost nothing at all."*

As I have said many times, when you are playing gambling machines, the vast majority of the time you will either hit the machine for a lot more wins than you should mathematically expect, and at other times for much less. Mathematics and math-based strategies are only a small *portion* of the overall strategies that make you a winner. Applying such strategies to video slots will not help you by themselves. While the firmware engineers will always deny that slots run in patterns, which we as players call "cycles," the fact remains that they freely admit that machines will not always run perfectly in accordance with a preset program. They can't, because if they did so they wouldn't be random. Consequently, we as players have far more tools at our disposal than math theorists and math-only strategy proponents give us credit for.

Knowing how to spot the better video slots, and how to spot the trends during which they pay more than their program allows, are the skills that *you* can learn (machines can't). You as a human player can do a lot more than trying to play as another machine. I like video slots because they are among the best-paying games in the casino. But when I say "best-paying games in the casino," you should understand that this is a qualified statement, and that it is intended for the comparisons among video slots, and not against games like blackjack; they are such vastly different games that trying to compare them would be like trying to

*Personal conversation with IGT engineers, Reno, Nevada.

fit a square peg into a round hole half its size. Among all slots and machine-based games, video slots are among the best paying, primarily for four main reasons:

1. They are new. Making them with better payback programs will attract more players to them and more players will become used to playing them.
2. They are "dollar" and "five dollar" and higher denomination games, even though they may have their base game unit credit value set at, say, a nickel. A nickel video slot machine that takes 45 coins is not a "nickel" machine. It is a $2.25 per pull machine and, therefore, classified among the "dollar slots" for our purposes. Since dollar and five-dollar slot machines are among the most liberal and best-paying slot machines on the casino floor, these games, too, will fall into these categories.
3. Video slots offer many paylines, resulting in many more frequent wins, thus diminishing the game's volatility index. The game will often support itself longer, without huge bankroll fluctuations, and will offer many wins more frequently. Although you will traditionally require a much larger bankroll than you may have estimated for a nickel slot machine because you are playing a "more than $2 machine," and therefore your bankroll should reflect that level of action.
4. Video slots offer many bonuses, and the entry to these bonus rounds can be achieved with great frequency. This is the primary reason why video slots can be such huge payers. Anytime you enter such a bonus round, you know you are already a winner. You can't lose. Many video slots have multiple bonuses, and within each of these there are multiple levels. Once there, you know you have a winning

event, and the only question that remains is just how big will your win be? Most of the time, these video slots will provide you with a very large win in such bonus rounds.

For these four main reasons, video slots offer some of the greatest enjoyment in gambling—the fun factor—and also provide some of the biggest pays for players who realize what these machines truly are and play them to the hilt and with the appropriate bankroll. *Selection* of the *kind* of machines will, therefore, become one of the most important skills you can learn and develop. Not all machines are the same, and not all games that look the same in fact are. There are many differences, some of them quite subtle. For example, some games may have five paylines, while other games that look identical will have nine paylines. The difference between these two machines, as based on the number of their paylines, can be staggering. The 5-line machine may have far fewer pays, and in lower amounts. Its top jackpot will also be lower, and the frequency of the entry to the bonus rounds may be less. The kinds of bonuses being offered can also be substantially reduced. The 9-line machine may require four more coins to play all lines, but the graduated investment is usually more than worth it. On this game—which may look identical to the 5-line version—there may be more bonuses. Entry into the bonuses may be easier, and certainly more frequent because you have four extra lines that can get you there. The pays may be bigger, and the frequency of hits greater. Because of the simple fact of adding four more lines to this version of that game, everything improves dramatically. While the 5-line game may have a top jackpot of, say, 12,500 coins, the 9-line version of the same game will most likely have a top jackpot of 50,000 coins, or more. That is four times the previous award, and makes sense because you are also wagering four more coins.

While most of the other pays are also likely to be increased by a factor of four, the increased frequency of hits makes it a much more valuable game. On this version of the game you will require a larger bankroll, because of the added extra wagers for the additional paylines, but this also results in many more pays, with greater value, and more chances to hit the bonuses for greater profits.

What is often lost among the various theories and analyses of slots, and particularly so for video slots, is the actual cash value of the wins—what I like to call the "money value." Remember this term and what it means, because you will see it again. What I call money value *is the actual value of the win relative to the investment required to get it.* When you hit a win of 50 coins, and it took you 45 coins to get it, the money value of that win is next to none. That extra five nickels you made isn't enough to go home with, and not much of a profit—even though, technically, it is a profit. Nonetheless, playing for these kinds of "profits" isn't the purpose, and shouldn't be the reason behind playing. This is akin to the kind of "grinding it out" approach that so many strategists advise as an approach to all gambling. Similarly, if you invest 25 coins on a nickel machine on a 5-line game, for a cost of $1.25 per spin, for a chance at a jackpot of 12,500 coins ($625), with odds of about 100,000 to 1 of hitting it, requiring a bankroll of about $200 for a good session, the money value of your win relative to the expenditure required, time dedicated to playing, and the odds against, simply isn't there. Let's say that you invested the $200 and were lucky enough to hit the $625 jackpot. Well, that's only a $425 profit, for a very long shot, with a large investment at stake. Now consider the same bankroll on a machine with nine lines, where the investment is $2.25 per spin, with a bankroll of $200, which is still a reasonable bankroll for these kinds of machines. Now the top jackpot is 50,000 coins, which is $2,500. You don't have to be a math genie to quickly understand that the difference here is $625 versus $2,500. This is a difference of $1,875 *more* value for the same win. Now the expenditure of the $200 bankroll makes sense, because if you do hit this pay, then your net is $2,500, minus the $200 bankroll, which equals $2,300 net gain. *That's* what I call money value, because that is serious take-home cash. Plus, of course, all of the other wins you may accumulate along the way, including some of the more frequent bonus wins that are likely to fuel your wins as you play.

Although you won't win that top jackpot each time you sit down with a stake of $200 for that session, the fact remains that by selecting this version of the two identical-looking machines, you are giving yourself the best chance at the bigger win, and that's what will generate your money value throughout play on video slots. The little pays in between, even pays of 1,000 coins and so on, aren't your money value profits—they are merely fuel for continued play. What does constitute money value are wins that actually substantially exceed the "coin value" of the wagers. On a 45-coin nickel machine, wins of 1,000 coins and 1,500 coins, and so on, are very frequent. They seem like big wins, but they are merely coin values and not money values. A hit of 1,000 nickels is only $50, and while it is a good hit, it isn't the "take the money and go home" win. There are, however, *cumulative* situations where even not hitting the biggest pay, or the second, or even third biggest pay, will *add up* to the "take the money and go home" wins. As you play video slots, and become familiar with them and their pay and play nuances, you will often hit a series of hits relatively close to each other in frequency. You will hit pays of 1,500 coins, 1,000 coins, 1,750 coins, 2,225 coins, and even 3,000 coins and more. Taken individually, with the possible exception of the 3,000-coin wins and up, these wins aren't the money value wins we look for in video slot play. They are

instead the continued fuel wins that allow us to keep playing. However, when they happen frequently, one after the
other, then, *viewed cumulatively*, they *together* make up what
should be our session-ending decision.

Let's assume that you will actually hit the very sequence
of wins that I just listed. This is not hard to do on the machines I will soon show you, and is in fact the exact and
identical sequence of pays that I hit on one such machine
just before writing this very paragraph! I hit this sequence
of pays within 15 pulls. This means that I had these huge
pays very close to one after the other, for a total 15-pull investment of 15 x $2.25 = $33.75. My total cumulative win
for these non-jackpot hits was 9,475 nickels, which equals
$473.75. Deduct from this the cost of those 15 spins—
$33.75—and my total money value win was $440. I started
that session with a $100 investment, which gave me the
starting credits value of 2,000 coin credits. At the time I hit
this sequence of non-jackpot cumulative pays, my credit
meter was at 2,750. This added a net of 750 credits to my
total win, which was an extra $37.50. So, when I cashed
out, I had the total of $440, plus my original $100, plus the
extra $37.50, for a gross of $577.50. Deduct the original investment of $100, and this left a net win of $477.50. In
about one hour of play for that session, the profit was 4.8
times over and above the initial starting bankroll, and all of
this without ever hitting any jackpot pay, and only one
bonus round (the 3,000-coin hit).

The point here is that even when *not* hitting the *top
jackpot*, or even not hitting any jackpots at all, and only
very nominal hits on the bonus rounds, the *cumulative effect* of many of these intermediate wins, at *maximum* coin
wagers, when happening relatively close to each other,
often results in the positive money value wins that are one
of the primary keys to winning at video slots. One of the
greatest money-making advantages of video slots is that you

don't have to hit the jackpot, and you don't have to hit the major pays, and you don't have to hit a lot of bonuses and a lot of secondary and tertiary tiered jackpots, but you can, and will, very often and quite frequently accumulate serious money very quickly by allowing yourself to hit a series of pays that, by themselves, wouldn't be much to go home with, but that *cumulatively add up* to a serious "take the money and go home with it" win. Maximizing your money value like this is important because it requires you to develop your observational skills to a finer edge. The reason most people lose when playing slots, and video slots, is that they play less-than-maximum coins and put back the wins they had. In the above example from my own recent wins, these events happened in fifteen minutes. Failing to recognize these events as a distinctly anomalous series, although in line with the expected probabilities in the parity of events model within the probability theory, would have resulted in an unwise player playing these wins back again. Parity of events simply means that, eventually, all the highs and lows will balance, and, therefore, the machine and its program will achieve statistical equivalence, and hold the stated percentage for the house. Therefore, when facing such a positive fluctuation such as the one I described, the converse will also be true and will happen equally as frequently. So, if you continue playing this money back, the chances are good that a converse sequence of equally negative situations will wipe out these wins, and that, therefore, parity had occurred and as a direct result you go home broke.

Video slots, and slots in general, can make huge money for the casinos because of the overwhelming ignorance of the players, their lack of understanding of the parity of events, and their lack of discipline. The oldest story in Las Vegas is this: It's easy to win money on slots—but it's hard to go home with it. Players don't think it's "enough," so they continue, and lose. If that's you, don't feel alone. It happens to everyone, even me. There have been times when I made an error in judgment, or failed in my own discipline, and as a result suffered a loss when I had already accumulated a money value win. It will happen to all of us, because we aren't perfect. My point is to make sure we are aware of these human failures and tendencies so that we can discipline ourselves to suffer from them only in the occasional lapse of concentration. These are observational skills that can be learned, and if you do so, you will be able to maximize your wins even on video slots—games that are classified by the math-only strategists as firmly in the "house game" category. The fact remains that they do pay, must pay, and that if you know which ones and how to spot this, you can make quite significant money value wins from them.

This brings me to the kinds of machines that are, in my opinion, the very best. As you read this book, you will see a selection of different machines and games. I have chosen to show you the very best of the lot—IGT games. IGT is the world's largest slot machine manufacturer. They make most of the games you will find in your favorite casino. About 80 percent of all the slot machines in the world are made by IGT, and they are, therefore, in my mind the standard by which all slot machines, and in particular video slot machines, should be judged. Although there are other machines made by other manufacturers, it is better to show you the best, so I have selected the biggest video slot machine manufacturer in the world, and from among their many hundreds of terrific games, selected the very best that they offer. I have consulted with IGT and their technicians and game developers to make sure that the games I am discussing are available and are in the top category of the most popular games. I consider these games to be the absolute pinnacle. The best games, the most fun, the best paying. There simply aren't any other machines and games that can compare to the innovative genius that went into the development of these

IGT machines. I have witnessed the process personally, and I am amazed at the great care that IGT takes in making these machines the fairest, best, and all around player friendly.

While other games may look similar, you will be well advised to look for the IGT logo on the machines in your favorite casino. If you see a machine that has the IGT logo, then you already know this is among the very best there is. Thereafter, look at the machines and games I show you in the chapters that follow, and compare the game to those I have listed here. If it is one of them, or it is similar, then it is one of the family of these great games that will not only provide you with lots of tremendous fun, but also with the best pays of any of their kind.

Video slots are the future of casino gaming, a future that is already here today. Learning how to spot the best games is the first thing you must learn in order to prepare yourself for winning at these games. Learning to look for the IGT games I have selected for this book is the first step in this process, and one most likely to assure you of the best games there are.

The Top 10 Video Slots

The video slot machines that I will show you in this chapter are the top 10 of all the video slots you will find in your favorite casino. What makes them the best? My books are written from the perspective of the *player*—the casino visitors, the customers, the people who actually go to the casinos to play these games and enjoy themselves. Although I could write about these games from the technical perspective, by pointing out some of the technological innovations and the pure marvel of them as a wondrous piece of workmanship and design, the simple fact remains that if they aren't good for the player, then what good are they? That's the primary reason why I have selected these machines to be in my Top 10 list. They are good, and by "good" I mean that they provide the player with the kind of experience that is both enjoyable and, quite often, also profitable. As a player, I look for machines that are interesting, innovative, offer a wide variety of pays, hit pays frequently, and the pays that they do hit are such as to provide what I had earlier called "money value." The engineers and designers at

IGT understood why people play slots, and have designed their games with the *players* in mind.

In choosing the top 10 games, I considered many criteria. The machines and games had to be new, they had to be fun, they had to be innovative, they had to have many paying features, such as bonuses that actually pay something worthwhile and hit often enough to warrant hitting them, that the machine or game had to provide decent money value wins and frequent hits that are actually made up of pays that matter, rather than just pays for the sake of hitting pays. Machines that are called "high-hit frequency" machines may not necessarily fall into the above categories. Just because a machine hits often doesn't mean that it's a good game. It depends on just precisely *what* the machine hits, and how much it is worth. The machines and games in my selection all provide high-hit frequency with very good and decent money value pays, and frequent and easy-to-hit and entertaining bonus rounds whose win values are substantial.

My other criterion for their selection was the theme. Are they somehow integrated into the American culture? What is it about them that could be easily identifiable? That's why you will see games like *Wheel of Fortune*®, *Beverly Hillbillies*™, *M*A*S*H*™, *American Bandstand*®, and so on. All of these are cultural icons of the twentieth and twenty-first American centuries, and are therefore easily identifiable. This has to do with "people appeal," and is one of the motivating factors behind the success of many games of this kind.

Finally I selected these machines and games, as indeed all the machines and games in this entire book, according to how well they pay. Many of these machines offer progressives, with some of them offering what is called "wide area progressives." These are machines like the great new *Video Megabucks*®, which is my number 9 game on this Top 10 list. These are the kinds of machines that you have already become used to with the traditional reel spinners like *Megabucks*® and *Quartermania*®. You will also see games like *Wheel of Fortune*®, which is my number 1 game on this list. Both *Video Megabucks*® and *Wheel of Fortune*® offer huge progressive awards for hitting the top jackpot. Players like to shoot for the big pays, and that's what drives the popularity of these area progressives. Unfortunately, many machines and games that are such progressives and offer such huge top jackpots are what's called "top-heavy," meaning that the majority of their payback is vested in these giant awards. One of the main reasons why both *Wheel of Fortune*® video version and the even newer *Video Megabucks*® have made this list is because they are *not* like that. These games actually provide you with steady pays throughout your play, not diminishing either the enjoyment of playing or the frequency and regularity of pays as you play. This is rare among video slots, and even rarer among traditional reel slots. I have played many slots in my time, including many of the very newest video slots, and have attended conventions where the really new slots and video slots are being shown, even years before they finally make it to the casinos. Frankly, there aren't many that I would call great.

As a direct result of all my research, I was able to pick these games with the full confidence in their value to you as a player, because I am also a player and I also play them, and not only in the boardrooms, test laboratories, or on the convention floor. I play these very games in the real casinos, for real money. I play then as I say they should be played, and I select their play based on the same advice and recommendations you are now reading. I like these games because they play well, and pay well. So, how do they play? Well, let's now start with the best of them. From top to bottom, here's my Top 10 list of the all-time best video slots, and how to play them.

WHEEL OF FORTUNE®

This is an incredibly popular game, and for good reason. Not only is this among the best paying games, but it is also great fun. Just about everybody who has been alive over the past 20 years knows about the TV game show of the same name, upon which this casino game is based. If you read my book *Powerful Profits from Slots,* you know how much I like the traditional reel-type slot machine, with the spinning wheel mounted at the top. That version of this game is called the Classic game, and was one of the very first games that included not only the bonus feature of the spinning bonus wheel, but also a link to a progressive. That game is also part of the IGT *MegaJackpots*™ system of linked progressives, meaning it is linked to a *MegaJackpots*™ progressive, and features a whole slew of extra bonuses and pays. While traditional reel-type slot machines do not generally have the physical capability of multiple lines and extra bonuses, the video version of *Wheel of Fortune®* is packed with features that are also quite profitable when hit. Photo 1 shows what this new video version of the game looks like.

1. The very popular *Wheel of Fortune®* video slot machine in the upright format.

As you can see, this new *Wheel of Fortune®* video slot machine is a tall game with a main video screen and a top mounted wheel very much like the one you may already have become used to from the now more traditional reel-type machine. Apart from the game itself, the main difference is the style of the game, the cabinet it's in, and the monitor. This is a brand new 19-inch IGT curved video monitor, set inside a very well-designed cabinet with a curved button deck. This makes the game very easy to operate, and the curved format and the angle of the screen help to prevent reflection from the casino lighting, which can cause eye fatigue when playing video machines. This is another of those "little things" that go into the design of the machine and affect your play and your winnings. Being able to play a game that is so well made as these new games and designs are allows you to have greater comfort at the game. Being able to play the game comfortably in turn allows you to remain at the game longer. Longevity of playing often leads to profits, because you will be able to put the game through more of its events. Of course, as you will see from the strategy sections later on, sometimes the best and most profitable course of play is to hit the machine quickly and then find another, but that isn't the point here. Many times, in order to maximize the win potential that these games offer, you will need to put the game through its paces for a little longer than most people would normally play. By being able to play on games such as these new designs, it will not be as tiring. You will have more time at the game. That will result in more spins, and these in more wins.

There are several versions of this new *Wheel of Fortune*® video slot machine, all of which can also be found in the *MegaJackpots*™ progressive link format wherever such are allowed under the gaming jurisdictions of that state, or country. Among these versions of the game are the traditional Classic format I mentioned in my earlier slots book, and also the new video versions that come in the Lucky Spin Triple Chance, and Extra Spin styles. The game I happen to mention here (shown in Photo 1), is the Extra Spin style. It is called Extra Spin because in one of the bonus events you can earn extra free spins. Here's how this bonus spins feature works: When you line up three or more of the "spin" icons on an active payline, from left to right, this will initi-

2. *Wheel of Fortune*® WHEEL letter bonus screen.

ate the Spin the Wheel bonus. The machine will then display a bonus screen that shows the now-familiar WHEEL letters. You can see what this bonus screen looks like in Photo 2.

Now you get to choose a letter. Touch the screen over any of the letters and that choice will reveal the number of spins of the wheel that you have won. This can be from as low as two spins to as many as seven. Each spin of the wheel will pay you anywhere from 10 times up to 250 times the value of your initiating credit bet. For example, if you are playing the maximum 5 credits per payline—which you should *always* do, because otherwise you can't win the jackpot—your wins will now be anywhere from 50 credits up to 1,250 per win. But that's not all. Now you can also earn extra spins. If you land on the slice of the wheel that shows the Extra Spin icon, these spins are added to your free spins. Hence the name of this version of the game: Extra Spin. Each time you land on that extra spin slice, this will add the original number of spins to your continuing spins. Let's say you have been awarded 10 spins. You have had 4 spins already, and on spin 5 you land on the Extra Spin slice (the "slice" is what is known as the "wedge" on the spinning wheel, over which the "rabbit's foot" comes to rest, thereby showing which is the winning event). Landing on that slice for those extra spins will add the full 10 spins back to your spin meter. You will start all over again with all 10 spins intact. If you don't land on any more Extra Spins, you will have had 15 total spins, even though you only earned 10 spins when you first landed on the bonus. But that isn't all! This can continue for as many times as you land on the Extra Spin slice, up to a total of 999 spins. You can easily see how this game can quickly turn a few dollars into many large wins, even without hitting the progressive jackpot.

Of course, hitting the progressive jackpot is what everybody plays for, and this game is no exception. If the casinos where you like to play are in a region of the United States, or the world, where the various gaming regulatory agencies allow such multi-link progressives, then you are likely to find this game with the IGT *MegaJackpots*™ system attached. This doesn't affect the game, other than to allocate a small percentage of the game to the growing progressive meter, just like all the other IGT progressives with which you may be familiar, like *Megabucks*® and *Quartermania*®. In those gaming jurisdictions that do not allow progressives, you can still find this game where the progressive jackpot symbols simply mean the top jackpot. That can be whatever amount the casino in that part of the country, or the world, will allow. Most of the casinos in the United States are in places where such progressive jackpots are allowed, and therefore it is simply easier for me to refer to this as the progressive jackpot, and progressive jackpot symbols, even though in some places these may in fact be non-progressive top-jackpot award symbols. Such non-progressive versions of this game are rare, so be aware that if the game you are seeing does not have a progressive meter display, such as the one shown on this version of the game in Photo 1, you are playing in a jurisdiction that has not yet allowed linked progressives. In that case, whenever you read the words "jackpot symbol" or "jackpot screen," or anything that has to do with a reference to such progressives, simply substitute the words "top jackpot," and that will be the same.

As with the traditional *Wheel of Fortune*® game, the jackpot and progressive jackpot symbols are the *Wheel of Fortune*® symbols. In this version of the game, these trigger the top jackpot, which is usually the progressive, when five of these symbols line up correctly on the ninth activated payline. This means that to win the top jackpot, you *must* play maximum coins and you must play *all* paylines. This is the best piece of advice I can give you for all of these video slot machines. If you do not do this you will never gain the maximum payback percentage of which these machines are capable, and you will also *never* be able to win the top jackpot or progressive. Remember this for all the games you read about in this book. Not one of these games will pay you back its optimum payback percentage, or allow you to get paid for the top and progressive jackpots, if you do not play maximum coins. This is to *your* advantage, because only by playing such maximum coins will you be able to make powerful profits from these great new machines and games. If you can't afford to play maximum coins, don't play. Save up your money, and play only when you can afford it. Playing these games for less than maximum coins will not entertain you, because it will waste your money. These great games are designed to be fun, and they can also be very profitable—but only if you play them properly. The machine's payback percentage is vested in the proper maximum coin play, because only then will you be able to trigger the machine's full payback for all the listed pays. If you play less than maximum coins, you will still be paid, and you will still win the top award if you are lucky enough to hit it, but you will not be able to win the progressive. Even on a non-progressive version of this game, or any of the other similar games, you will not be paid the maximum award that the game is capable of paying.

I have not written this book to show you how to be entertained by *losing* your money. I want to show you these games, and how to play them *to your best advantage*, and that means first and foremost to only play them with the maximum wager in order to make the game pay you what it is designed to pay, and capable of paying. A win of 10,000 credits for 1-coin play may be fine for you, and possibly exciting, but a win of $250,000 for a 5-coin bet for the same event, or more, is a lot better and a whole lot more money value. I hope you get the point, because if you still go and play these games for less than maximum coins, then my efforts to help you make profits have been wasted. You can't make profits from these games if you don't play maximum coins. You may be entertained by these great games, but you will be a loser. That's a plain fact. I sure hope you won't allow yourself to fall into this pit of trying to "save" money by gambling badly.

These new versions of the *Wheel of Fortune*® video slots come in a 9-line format. This means that you must make a

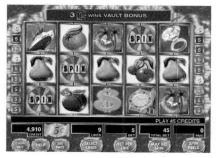

wager on all nine lines, and with maximum coins for all lines. So, you will be wagering 45 coins per spin, on most of these games. You can see what the main 9-line screen on this machine looks like in Photo 3, and the main jackpot win on the Top Award screen in Photo 4.

3. Nine-line main game screen for *Wheel of Fortune*®.

The *Wheel of Fortune*® jackpot symbols on these video versions of the game are circular, while on the traditional reel-type slot machine they are more square in design. This doesn't affect the game itself, because the way the symbols are presented doesn't mean any-

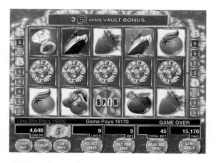

4. Top Award screen for *Wheel of Fortune*®.

thing to the machine or game. However, if you are not familiar with the traditional game, it is perhaps important to let you know what those symbols look like, because they are not only the jackpot symbols on this new video game, but also act as Wild and Doubler symbols. With the exception of the Vault, Gold Dollar, and Spin symbols, or any other *Wheel of Fortune*® symbols, these jackpot symbols will substitute for all the other symbols, as a Wild replacement. Therefore, when you hit one or more of these symbols in a combination that is not a jackpot, but is lined up with other paying symbols on the game, these *Wheel of Fortune*® symbols will substitute for those others and make a winner. In addition, such a winner is also doubled. This doesn't substitute for the others as listed here because those are the bonus symbols, and, of course, all five of the *Wheel of Fortune*® symbols make the jackpot, so they don't need to substitute for each other.

I have already mentioned the WHEEL Spin bonus; now it is time to mention the other two bonuses that are available on this new video game. The first is the Gold Dollar bonus, which is a "scatter" screen. You can see what this looks like in Photo 5.

In Photo 5 you see the Gold Dollar bonus screen, and there you will see three golden $$$ symbols. These large golden dollar symbols work as a scatter pay whenever three or more show up on the screen. You can win up to 200 times your line bet, but that isn't the best news. The best news is that these scatters pay *in addition* to any other line pays. This means that when you hit a pay on any of the paylines,

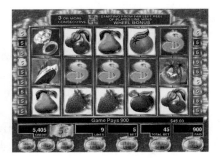

5. Gold Dollar bonus screen for *Wheel of Fortune*®.

or more pays on many paylines which also happens often on this game, and you also get the scatters along with those pays, you will be paid for *everything* cumulatively. On some other games, particularly many of the games that are not IGT games, you will often find that you don't get paid for some of the wins when you hit the scatters, or vice versa. On this game, your wins multiply, even with the scatters hit. And finally, there's the Vault bonus. You can see what this looks like in Photo 6.

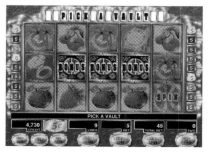

Whenever you hit three Vault symbols in *any position* on the adjacent reels two through four (the middle three reels), you will be taken to the Vault bonus. There you will be asked to select one of the three vaults. You do this by touching your finger to the screen over the one you wish to choose.

6. Vault bonus screen for *Wheel of Fortune®.*

Once you make that selection, the machine will display the amount of your win, which is a credit multiplier. You can win anywhere from 5 times up to 25 times your line bet wager.

Well, that's about it for the terrific *Wheel of Fortune®* video slot machine. I also want to mention that this game is available as a slant-top model, which is a smaller machine mounted on an angle so that you can sit at it. There's a small table in front of you, with the machine mounted on a slight "slant" in front of you, hence the industry name for such machines being "slant-tops." It's the same machine and game, and it has all of the features as I have described them here. Personally, I do not like slant-tops; they tend to be very uncomfortable. I prefer the nice, clean, tall machine, particularly these new IGT cabinets with the curved button deck and the great new 19-inch monitor, as shown in Photo 1. Now I will move on to my second best game of the top 10, which is *Jeopardy!*®

JEOPARDY!®

This is another of the famous television shows that have become a video slot machine. There have been several versions of the *Jeopardy!*® slot machine, including a reel machine and an earlier version of this video game. I will show you the two latest incarnations of *Jeopardy!*®, one called the *Tournament of Champions*™, and the other the *Free Spin*™.

Jeopardy! Tournament of Champions™

This is a 9-line, 45-coin maximum wager game, loaded with ways to win. There are, again, different configurations of the game, including the tall one and the sit-down game called a slant-top. Although I prefer the tall ones, the latest trend is in slant-tops, so I will show you that one in Photo 7.

The bonus starts when three or more *Tournament of Champions*™ symbols land from left to right on an active payline. The game then takes you to a life-like rendition of the TV game show, and TV host Alex Trebek introduces six categories. After you select a category, this then reveals a

7. The slant-top version of the new *Jeopardy! Tournament of Champions*™.

column full of bonus credits. If you uncover a Daily Double symbol on one of the monitors in the column, the game

8. *Tournament of Champions*™ bonus screen for *Jeopardy!*®

doubles your winnings for the round. Play continues until you find a Bonus Complete symbol, which ends the bonus game, or a Double symbol, which starts the Double round of bonus game play. You can see what this bonus screen looks like in Photo 8.

In the Double Jeopardy round, Alex Trebek introduces a new set of categories from which to pick. You select more categories in the search for more bonus credits, and hope to avoid the Bonus Complete symbol while looking for more Daily Double symbols and the coveted Final symbol, which launches the lucrative Final bonus round. To see what the Double Jeopardy bonus screen looks like, see Photo 9.

9. Double Jeopardy bonus screen.

In the Final bonus round, you select one of four question marks. The symbol reveals a bounty of bonus credits that will make you feel like a true champion. Photo 10 shows this final bonus screen.

Naturally, to win the top jackpot you need to hit the correct combination of the winning symbols. When five of the *Jeopardy!*® jackpot symbols land on the ninth payline with

10. Final bonus round screen for *Jeopardy!*®

a maximum bet, you win a *MegaJackpots*™ top award of at least $100,000. This is paid *instantly* upon verification of win, so you don't have to wait for any annuities. Vivid re-creations of the set, authentic theme music from this wildly popular television game show, and the voice of host Alex Trebek combine to make a package you're sure to recognize. There's no question about it. This video slots game answers your need for exciting game play.

Jeopardy! Tournament of Champions™ *Free Spin*

And the answer is—the newest video slot game that's based on one of television's most popular game shows. And the question is—what is *Jeopardy!*® video slots *Tournament of Champions Free Spi*n™ game that is the latest addition to this exciting family of games?

The *Jeopardy!*® video slots *Tournament of Champions Free Spin*™ game offers you the chance to win big. This 9-line, 45-coin game is loaded with ways to win. Although at first sight this game may look almost identical to the game I have just shown you, it is actually quite different. While the *Jeopardy!*® theme is the same, the game plays differently and offers different bonuses. The first difference you will find is that this is not a progressive. That's why this is called the Free Spin, because here you get to spin the reels for free in that bonus round, but the top jackpot is a fixed amount and not a progressive meter. The difference is actually in the game content itself, rather than the overall game, because this game is still based on the same IGT platform for which these games have been designed. You will, however, win more often on this version of the game as compared to

11. *Jeopardy! TOC™* Free Spin video slot machine in the slant-top format.

the progressive, simply because the progressive jackpot doesn't hit as often as do more traditional non-progressive jackpots. Although the game can look almost identical to the others, you can tell the difference by looking for the progressive jackpot meter. If the game does *not* have the jackpot meter, then it is this game, the one I am now writing about. If it *does* have a jackpot meter, it is the game I have just shown you, above. It's really that simple. You can help yourself make better playing choices by learning to spot differences like that. To see what this game looks like, see Photo 11. Be sure not to confuse it with the one shown in Photo 7, because they seem to look the same. Look closer, and you will see that they are *different* machines.

On this game, the Free Spin bonus starts when three or more *Tournament of Champions*™ symbols land from left to right on an active payline. The game then takes you to a life-like rendition of the game show set. You start with three free spins and a bonus multiplier value of one. Alex Trebek prompts you to select from the monitors on the screen. Each selection increments the number of bonus spins or adds to the multiplier value. The game launches the Free Spin portion of the bonus when you find the Begin Free Spins symbol. The reels spin and land in a whirlwind of action.

12(a). Multiplier selection screen.

Winning symbol combinations are multiplied by the multiplier value. If no winning combinations land on the reels, you are awarded three times the line bet, then further multiplied times the multiplier amount. The screen displays the bonus jackpot when the free spins are complete. To see what all these bonus screens look like, look at Photos 12(a) through 12(c).

Of course, there is the top jackpot. Some of these versions of the game may have the *MegaJackpots*™ progressive, but the game I am describing here does not. The jackpot happens when five *Jeopardy!*® symbols land on the ninth payline with a maximum bet, and if this happens to you, you win the top award. Depending on the casino where you are playing, this top jackpot may vary, but tradi-

12(b). Multiplier summary screen.

tionally it will be at least $100,000. Both of these versions of the game are great fun to play, and many of the bonuses and straight line pays offer terrific wins, with substantial money value.

12(c). Free Spin, Bonus Spin, and Multiplier summary screen.

Now I want to take you to the hills of Beverly, for some fun with a bunch of hillbillies.

BEVERLY HILLBILLIES™

This is another great television show that has become a winning video slot machine. The "theming" of video slots used to be something that manufacturers didn't think would work. Slot machine makers, and casinos, used to think that people wouldn't identify with anything that didn't look like the traditional reel spinning slot machine. But with the advances in computer technology that have made video slots possible, it was a natural evolution to make these video slot machines "themed," and linked to something with which most people would identify. Classic TV shows are a natural for this sort of gaming evolution, and that's why we now see so many new video slots tied to these great old shows.

Like most people who grew up in the 1960s, I was a great fan of the *Beverly Hillbillies*™ television show. Not so long ago I was able to meet with Max Baer Jr., the actor who played Jethro on the show. It was a great thrill for me, not only because I enjoyed the television show so much, but also because it was at the gaming convention where all these great new video slots were being presented for the first time. At industry conventions I get to see some of the greatest video slots long before they make it to the casinos. Some of these games are still in development when I see them for the first time, and changes often happen between the time they are shown at the industry convention, and the time you get to play them. Mostly this is because the developers want to make sure that everything that can be done to make this playing experience terrific for you, the casino player, is done before you get to play these new games, in order to prevent any problems. The process that these machines go through to verify and test their accuracy is tremendously complicated, and much more is done to ensure that you are comfortable at the game, from the design of the cabinetry to the game console itself. There's a lot of careful thought being given to these games, much more so than the mere theme of the game. These versions of the *Beverly Hillbillies*™ video slots from IGT are among the most popular games you will find in the casino. There are three versions— *Clampett's Cash*, *Bubblin' Crude*™, and *Moonshine Money*, all of which are progressives (where such progressives are available and permitted by the regulatory agencies). *Clampett's Cash* features Jed Clampett as the main theme character. Jethro is featured in *Bubblin' Crude*™, and dear old Granny is featured in *Moonshine Money*. I will now tell you more about how these games work, in turn, beginning with *Clampett's Cash*.

The Beverly Hillbillies™—Clampett's Cash

Come along with Jed, Jethro, Elly May, and Granny and live the high life with this great new video slot machine. The

game features 15 lines and is packed with bonus game play. The progressive award gives you a gaming experience bigger than a well of bubbling crude oil. You can't miss the machines, because they are quite tall and many of them have a statue of Jed holding wads of cash. You can see what this version of the machine looks like in Photo 13.

There are several different bonuses available. The main bonus starts when three *Clampett's Cash* symbols land from left to right on an active pay-

13. *Beverly Hillbillies*™ *Clampett's Cash* video slot machine.

14(a). Jed's Vault.

line. Jed then takes you to his secret vault for a chance at some serious loot. There you have 14 tries to determine the four-digit combination to the vault. Even if you can't crack the code and don't open the safe, you still win a nice payout, and the bonus ends there. But if you do crack the vault, and it opens, you get to keep any leftover picks and receive two more for good measure. You then get to select that number of safety deposit boxes and receive the riches inside. You can follow the action in the top box as each value is revealed. The values are totaled and multiplied by the line bet for a win that would make Jed proud. You can see what these two bonus screens look like in Photos 14(a) and 14(b).

14(b). Safety Deposit Boxes.

The next bonus happens when three, four, or five Wizard of Wall Street symbols land from left to right on an active payline, where you will be whisked off to the Street bonus by investment counselor Jed. You will receive five bills to invest in your choice of 16 ventures, from gold bars to stocks to cattle ranches. Then, you select an investment for each bill. Each investment reveals a value that is multiplied by the dollar amount of the bill for a credit win. With your successful investment in place, you will roll in dough as the credits from all of the investments are added to the meter. You can see this bonus screen in Photo 15.

15. Wizard of Wall Street bonus.

Naturally, the jackpot happens when five of the *Beverly Hillbillies*™ symbols land on payline 15 with a maximum bet. If that happens for you, you will win a jackpot of at least $100,000 (paid instantly upon verification of win). Even Mr. Drysdale would be impressed by that! With authentic sounds and life-like voiceovers playing on the enhanced sound system, and a variety of comical game play options, you are sure to want to gather around the game and sit a spell. The next two versions of this game are similar, yet different, each in its own special way.

The Beverly Hillbillies™— Moonshine Money

This is also a 15-line game, with a progressive jackpot full of that sweet backwoods moonshine money. Apart from the traditional designs, this game is available in a tall slant-top, a slant-top with arched top box, and an upright. The tall slant-top features a moving topper with Granny in her rocking chair. You will easily recognize this classic television image and

16. *Beverly Hillbillies*™ *Moonshine Money* video slot machine.

the original theme music that plays throughout the game on the enhanced sound system that comes with all these IGT video slots. You can see what this game looks like in Photo 16.

The main bonus is triggered when three Moonshine Money symbols land from left to right on an active payline. When Granny fires up the still you can follow the action

17(a). Granny's Brew Screen Still.

from the Brew screen. The contraption pours the brew into various containers. Each drop in each container is worth a value, which is combined with the values from the other containers and multiplied by the line bet for the total award. Granny brews up four batches of credits, and the possible win amounts are displayed on the bonus meter on the screen. The still explodes when it's pushed beyond its limits, and you then receive the biggest award of the four that were poured. You will love the 100-proof credits that roll up on the meter, because this bonus really packs a punch! You can see what these bonus screens look like in Photos 17(a) and 17(b).

17(b). Brew Again bonus screen.

The next bonus is based on one of the most popular episodes of this classic show, the Giant Jackrabbit. This bonus is triggered when three or more Giant Jackrabbit symbols land left to right on an active payline. You then get to hunt for the animal anomaly in the Clampett mansion by trying to catch the critter.

18(a). Giant Jackrabbit introduction screen.

You do this by touching the screen when the rabbit's ears appear from behind pieces of furniture. If you miss, the game awards a credit value or displays a Next Room symbol, which indicates the animal's escape to another room. When you come too close for comfort, the rabbit raises the white flag in surrender and the game awards more bonus credits. The total win is added to the meter when the bonus ends. Photos 18 (a) and 18 (b) show these bonus screens.

Naturally, the top jackpot is again paid when five *Beverly Hillbillies*™ symbols land on payline 15 with a maximum bet. If that happens you win a jackpot of at least $100,000, paid instantly upon verification of the win. This exciting game is also available as a penny denomination game, and is

18(b). Giant Jackrabbit bonus screen.

designed specifically for the EZ Pay™ Ticket System that lets you play without the need for coins. The final version of these great games is the one with Jethro as the main character, called the *Bubblin' Crude*™.

The Beverly Hillbillies™—Bubblin' Crude™

Here comes more game play based on *The Beverly Hillbillies*™. The *Bubblin' Crude*™ video slot—the latest addition

to the TV Hits series of games—showcases the characters of this hilarious show. Five reels of video action are available in a 15-line, 150-coin penny game or a 15-line, 75-coin nickel version. This is also a *MegaJackpots Instant Winners™* progressive, when such are available in the gaming jurisdiction where your favorite casino is located. Photo 19 shows what this game looks like.

The game also features two entertaining bonuses, and a scatter pay based on classic humor from the hit TV comedy, along with animation and well-known music from the popular television show. The "scatter" pays happen when two to five scattered Hound Dog symbols show up anywhere on the screen; this will then pay you up to 400 credits. These are further multiplied by the total wager. But the main bonus fun happens with the two bonus screens.

19. *Beverly Hillbillies™ Bubblin' Crude™* video slots.

Jethro's Vittles™ bonus is triggered when the *Jethro's Vittles™* symbol lands in the middle position of the third reel. You then make one to five selections from the various critter symbols on the screen, and each selection pays 1 to 10 credits, multiplied by times the total initiating bet. You can see this bonus screen in Photo 20.

20. *Jethro's Vittles™* bonus screen.

Bubblin' Crude™ bonus is launched when three, four, or five *Bubblin' Crude™* symbols land from left to right on an active payline. You are then prompted to place oil derricks on the Clampett property, after which the derricks overflow with bonus credits. You can win up to 1,250 credits, further multiplied by the initiating line bet. This screen is shown in Photo 21.

Of course the top jackpot happens when five *Beverly Hillbillies*™ symbols land on payline 15 with a maximum bet on all paylines. The game then pays you an Instant Winners top jackpot, which can be a progressive if such are allowed in the region where you are playing. If this is

21. *Bubblin' Crude*™ bonus screen.

not a progressive, the stand-alone game's top jackpot is up to 10,000 credits, multiplied times the line bet. So, if you are playing 5 credits per line, and the game you are playing is not a progressive, you will win 50,000 credits. Not a bad win, in anyone's language!

*M*A*S*H*™

I remember when *M*A*S*H*™ first came on television as if it was yesterday. I also remember the movie, which I found to be incredibly funny at the time, way back in 1970. The early years of the television show were equally hilarious, and I watched the whole 10 years' worth of shows on TV, and then watched them all again, many times over in reruns. In 2003 I had the opportunity to meet Radar O'Reilly (played so perfectly by actor Gary Burghoff) at a gaming convention in Las Vegas. Unashamedly I was a fan, and I got his autograph. He is as nice and as funny in person as his character was on *M*A*S*H*™. As with the other great television show themes, IGT developed a video slot machine based on the *M*A*S*H*™ television series. All of your favorite TV characters from that show are mentioned, and all are part of this video slot game that is also a progressive. I am pleased to be able to show you this game and tell you all about it. It is sure to be one of the most popular casino games.

*M*A*S*H*™ Video Slots

22. *M*A*S*H*™ video slot machine in the slant-top format.

Welcome to the 4077th, home of the *M*A*S*H*™ video slot! This 15-line, 150-coin *iGame-Plus*™ penny denomination game beckons you to sit down for a drink at the Officers' Club and to visit with the occupants of the Swamp. Part of our TV Hits series of games, the *M*A*S*H*™ game features reel symbols that pay tribute to the characters of the ground-breaking television comedy. Attention. Attention. Players are lining up for a seat at the *M*A*S*H*™ video slot. With penny game play and an amazing spinning wheel and reel in the top box, you will stand up and salute when you see this game. A trip to the O.R. has never been so much fun. You can see what this game looks like in Photo 22.

This game also pays several bonuses, as well as a scatter pay. The scatter pay happens when three, four, or all five Helmet symbols appear anywhere in the window, on any reel, and in any position. You will be paid a multitude of credits, which is sure to fund a long evening of drinking at Rosie's Bar. This Helmet Scatter Pay feature is shown in Photo 23.

23. Helmet Scatter Pay bonus screen.

The game then requests your presence at bonus headquarters in the Super Spin bonus, which is triggered when three Sign symbols land from left to right on an active payline. You are then prompted to select one of the three symbols to determine the number of spins of the wheel in the top box. The wheel spins and lands on a credit value, which is multiplied by the line bet. If the wheel lands on a Super Spin slice, the top-box reel takes command. The reel spins and lands on a credit value from 75 to 1,000 credits, which is also multiplied by the initiating line bet. The bonus continues until you run out of wheel spins. Now that's a jackpot worthy of celebration. How about a three-day pass to Tokyo? You can see what the Super Spin bonus screen looks like in Photo 24.

Of course the top jackpot happens when all five *M*A*S*H*™ symbols land on payline 15 with the maximum bet wagered. You then get to take home the linked-progressive *MegaJackpots Instant Winners*™ jackpot, as available in the jurisdiction where your favorite casino is located. This exciting penny denomina-

24. Super Spin bonus screen for *M*A*S*H*™ video slots.

tion game is designed specifically for the *EZ Pay*™ Ticket System, or a tokenized casino. With a variety of game play that's better than anything the mess tent could offer, I think you'll agree that the *M*A*S*H*™ video slot gives you the "best care anywhere."

ADDAMS FAMILY™

The very popular *Addams Family*™ cartoon characters have also been a staple of the current pop culture for many years. I discussed this game in some detail in my book *Powerful Profits from Slots*, so I will here concentrate only on showing you the new version that you can now play in your favorite casino. That game is what's called a "stand-alone" game, which is not a progressive, called *Cousin It*™. The one that's just called *The Addams Family*™ is the progressive version of this game theme.

The Addams Family™—Cousin It™ Video Slots

More creepy, kooky, spooky fun is headed your way with

the latest and hairiest addition to the IGT video slots family. This game is a 5-reel, 9-line, 45-coin nickel game with all the features you have come to expect from video slots, including rich computer animation, familiar theme music, an optional Lurch or Uncle Fester topper, and a stunning top-box design that stands out in a crowd. You can see what this game looks like in Photo 25.

25. *Addams Family™ Cousin It™* video slots.

A variety of hairdo symbols—including beehives, Afros, pigtails, and more—appear on the reels and when two or more Scissors symbols land anywhere on the screen, this scatter pay slashes the credit meter, adding sharp bonus credits. When three Good Hair Day symbols land on reels one, two, and three of a played line, it's time for stylish bonus game action in *Cousin It's*™ a Good Hair Day bonus. A minimum of 10 bonus spins are played on all 15 lines, as each spins automatically washes over the screen. Randomly selected bonus multipliers along the bottom of the screen lather up to 15 times the bonus win for each spin! But the *Cousin It*™ money-making makeover isn't over yet. If three, four, or five scattered Good Hair Day symbols appear during the bonus round, 10 more bonus spins are awarded! With each spin a potential

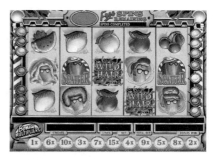

26. Good Hair Day bonus screen for *Cousin It*™ video slots.

winner, credit values pile up as the bonus round progresses. The bubbling bonus game ends when zero free spins remain, but you can win up to 510 free spins! You can see this bonus screen in Photo 26.

Of course the object of any slot machine is to pay you the top jackpot. On this game, you will win the top award when five *Addams Family*™ symbols land on the ninth payline with a maximum bet. When that happens, the game pays you the top award of 50,000 credits. So, don't be scared to win it!

DIAMOND CINEMA®

I first introduced the *Diamond Cinema®* series of video slots in my book *Powerful Profits from Slots*, where I showed the Marilyn Monroe and the Bogart and Bergman series. Those games have become so popular that IGT introduced several new models. Among these are three brand new video slots featuring Frank Sinatra, Steve McQueen, and one featuring the original "rebel," the late teen idol and actor James Dean.

Diamond Cinema® Featuring *Frank Sinatra™ Gift Wheel™* Video Slots

Start spreading the news! This 5-reel, 15-line, 75-coin nickel game puts you on top of the heap—the king of the hill. And no one is better suited to take them there than the Chairman of the Board himself. So, make way for the million-dollar machine! This is an eye-catching, stunning video slot machine, easily identified with the signature "Sinatra" logo on top of the machine's display cabinet. It is available both as a *MegaJackpots™* linked-progressive jackpot game (where available), and stand-alone version that has a fixed jackpot. You can see what this game looks like in Photo 27.

There are two bonuses, called the *Gift Wheel™* and *Dice™* .The first bonus, the *Gift Wheel™*, is initiated by three wheel symbols on reels one, two, and three of a played line. You then choose your favorite

27. *Frank Sinatra™ Gift Wheel™* video slots.

Sinatra song to reveal the number of wheel spins. This then spins the top counted wheel, similar to the *Wheel of Fortune*® game, where you can win anywhere from 10 to 100 times the initiating line bet. Plus, if you land on the Gift slice, that offers you the chance to choose

28(a). *Sinatra*™ *Gift Wheel*™ bonus.

an on-screen gift box for even more credits. The *Dice*™ bonus is triggered by three or more dice symbols in any position on the reels. You then choose an on-screen dice symbol to reveal a credit amount, at which point a video clip shows Frank rolling dice to multiply the on-screen dice credit amount. You can see what both these bonus screens look like in Photos 28(a) and 28(b).

28(b). *Sinatra*™ *Dice*™ bonus.

Naturally, the top jackpot happens when five *Sinatra*™ marquee symbols land on pay-line 15 with maximum bet wagered. This then pays the *Diamond Cinema*® linked-progressive jackpot (where available), or the top award in stand-alone versions. The next version of this game features a Record wheel bonus.

Diamond Cinema® Featuring *Frank Sinatra*™
Sinatra Record™ Video Slots

Roll out the red carpet—the million-dollar voice has arrived! This 5-reel, 15-line, 75-coin nickel game transports you down memory lane accompanied by the sights and sounds of this legendary superstar. With two eye-catching topper designs—the *Sinatra*™ signature marquee or the *Diamond Cinema*® movie marquee—this game has no trouble standing out in a crowd. You will adore listening as "Ol' Blue Eyes" serenades you through the enhanced stereo

sound with many of the songs that made him famous. The *Frank Sinatra*™ video slots *Record Wheel* game is offered as part of the *Diamond Cinema*® linked-progressive jackpot (in jurisdictions where *Mega-Jackpots*™ linked-progressives are available), as well as in the stand-alone version, and all these machines are manufactured for simple conversion to the *EZ Pay*™ Ticket System. Photo 29 shows the *Diamond Cinema*® version.

Like the previous game, this one also offers several bonuses. The Expanding Wild Feature asks you to keep your eyes on the reel symbol featuring *Sinatra*™ in a tuxedo. When it lands on the second or fourth reel, it expands to make the entire reel wild, and pays all winning combinations. Now that's one sweet deal! The *Record Deal*™ bonus starts when you line up three Gold Record symbols on reels one, two, and three of a played line, and this then initiates the

29. *Sinatra Record*™ video slots in the *Diamond Cinema*® series.

Record Deal™ bonus game. You get to press the on-screen Spin button to activate the big bonus wheel. Playing much like a board game, the number indicated by the wheel is the number of spaces the game moves clockwise around the circle of on-screen *Sinatra*™ albums. You win the number of credits indicated on albums on which the game lands. If the wheel lands on a "$" symbol,

30(a). Expanding Wild Feature screen.

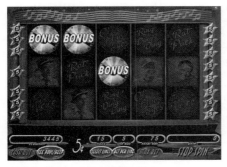

30(b). *Record Deal*™ initiator screen.

then you win *all* the values indicated on albums from the current You Are Here position to the next album featuring the word Collect. If there are no albums with the word Collect appearing on the screen, you win *all* values listed on the board. The *Record Deal*™ bonus continues, with accruing credits, until the game lands on an album with the word Collect. You can see the three bonus screens in Photos 30(a) through 30(c).

Of course the top jackpot is paid when five *Sinatra*™ signature marquee symbols line up on the fifteenth payline with maximum credits wagered, upon

30(c). *Record Deal*™ bonus screen.

verification of the win, either as a fixed jackpot or the progressive where available.

Diamond Cinema® Video Slots Featuring *Steve McQueen*™

You will like living the fast life of car chases and motorcycle races with the latest release in the *Diamond Cinema*™

series (see photo 31). This 5-reel, 15-line, 75-coin game is sure to spark an adrenaline rush equal to the likes of the legendary movie tough guy himself—*Steve McQueen*™. So, buckle up for the ride of your life! This game is also available as an IGT *MegaJackpots*™ linked-progressive (in approved jurisdictions), or as a set-amount top award for stand-alone games. In addition to the other features, the *Diamond Cinema*™ symbol matches all other symbols, acting as a wild match symbol, except for the *Fast Cash*™ and *Ride to Win*™ bonus symbols.

The *Fast Cash*™ bonus is initiated by *Fast Cash*® bonus symbols on reels one, two, and three of a played line. Good Guy Steve chases the Bad Guy in an on-screen car chase, and you get to select an escape exit for each car chase. Credits are awarded for each police badge collected by Steve during the chase and its outcome. The *Ride to Win*™ bonus is initiated by three or more *Ride to Win*™ bonus symbols on a played line. You then choose one on-screen "destination" symbol to reveal credits awarded. The bonus win doubles if the motorcycle rider ends his ride at the chosen destination. Photos 32(a) and 32(b) show these bonus screens.

31. *Diamond Cinema*® *Steve McQueen*™ video slots.

32(a). *Fast Cash*™ bonus screen.

The Top Reel Award, which is the jackpot, is paid when all five *Diamond Cinema*® symbols land on the first payline with max credits bet.

And now for the last in this new series of video slots under the Diamond Cinema banner, the *James Dean*™ game.

Diamond Cinema® Video Slots Featuring *James Dean*™

32(b). *Ride to Win*™ bonus screen.

James Dean was a teen idol in the 1950s. He only made three movies, but two of them have become classics of modern American cinema. They were *Rebel Without a Cause*, and *Giant*, the latter with Rock Hudson and Elizabeth Taylor. Shortly after filming was completed on the movie *Giant*, James Dean died in a car crash while driving his favorite sports car along a road north of Hollywood. His early death and unfulfilled potential as an actor struck hard. People the world over mourned him, and generations of teenagers and young adults idolized him. He was the original rebel, the original hip-hop star. Although many people in this day and age may no longer remember him, or know much about him, he is still part of the American pop culture, and very much the source of the "modern," or "mod" style that today's young adults find so alluring. When you see music videos of young performers, including pop, hip-hop, and rap, all of them find their original inspiration in James Dean, whether or not they know it, or realize it.

Now, as part of the *Diamond Cinema*® series of video slots, IGT has brought the image of James Dean back to life in this great new slot machine. The game comes in two styles, one with James Dean in his leather jacket, as "The Rebel," and the other with his cowboy hat in character from the movie *Giant*. The first is usually found as the tall stand-alone game, while the second is the slant-top. Both versions of the game offer the same playing structure and bonuses; the differences are only in the presentation of the game. You can find them easily by the movie marquee at the top of the machine, where it says: *James Dean™ starring in the Million Dollar Heist* (see Photo 33).

The game is a 5-reel, 15-line game, and offers two bonuses and a scatter pay. This scatter pay is a simple symbol which says appropriately, "scatter" on it. The first bonus starts when you hit three or more Oil Derricks. You are then prompted to pick one derrick which then explodes and shows you the credit value. The more Oil Derricks that land on your reels, the more choices you will get. The second bonus starts when three or more Race Car symbols land left to right on any active pay-

33. *James Dean™ Million Dollar Heist* video slots.

line. When this happens, the game takes you to the Free Spin Rally bonus, where you get 15 free spins at twice the payoff, except for the top jackpot, which will only pay its stated award and will not be doubled when hit during this bonus round. All other pays are paid at

33(a). *James Dean*™ Scatter pay screen.

twice the amount, so this is a really great bonus. But that's not all. While in this bonus round of 15 free spins at twice

the pay you also happen to hit the Oil Derricks bonus, you get to pick more credits as well as have the chance to earn more free spins if three or more of the Race Car symbols also happen to land on one of your active paylines during this bonus round.

33(b). Oil Derricks bonus screen.

All of these pays add up, and that's what makes this particular game and bonus round truly a money value game. You can see what these bonus screens look like in Photos 33(a) through 33(c).

As with all the games in the *Diamond Cinema*®

33(c). Free Spins Rally bonus screen.

series, the top jackpot is paid when all five of the *Diamond Cinema®* jackpot symbols land on any active payline. The amount of this jackpot depends on the jurisdiction where your casino is located, but it will mostly be commensurate with the jackpots found among the other games in this series.

AMERICAN BANDSTAND®

Many young players may not remember how huge the television music show *American Bandstand®* once was. It was an icon of American television and popular music. Now those of us who remember that show can relive that excitement through this new IGT video slot machine. Younger players, who may not know the show can get into the excitement of it through this game. So come top the charts with the *American Bandstand®* video slot machine. You will be sure to dance the night away while playing this game and listening to the hits of the '50s, '60s, '70s, and '80s. The be-bopping bonus games for this 5-reel, 20-line theme provide easy and fun ways for you to earn additional credits. This is a very tall and very distinctive game, and you won't be able to miss it in the casino. It is topped with the AB symbol for *American Bandstand®*, and also with a spinning wheel similar to the *Wheel of Fortune®* game, but with the record twist (Chubby Checker would be proud!) appropriate for this game (see Photo 34).

There are two bonuses available with this game. The first is the Rate a Record bonus. When a Rate a Record symbol lands on reels one, two, and three of a played line, the bonus starts. You are presented with a popular song title from four decades of music and asked to select one of the four songs. The game then reveals a number of bonus wheel spins. Wheel spins always grant credits, but if the bonus wheel lands on a gold or platinum selection, you get to se-

34. The *American Bandstand®* video slot machine.

lect buttons on the screen that award additional credit values. The second bonus is the Top Ten bonus. The countdown to bonus game excitement begins when a Top Ten symbol lands on reels one, two, and three of a played line and the bonus hits the air. You will be asked to select a record to reveal the song's chart position (number of bonus credits) for week one. You can then track the song as it moves up and down the chart for a total of five weeks (five chances), or you can choose to stop and collect the winnings. The higher the song rates on the music chart, the bigger the win. The top jackpot is usually in the range of 50,000 credits, and is awarded when all five of the jackpot symbols land on any active payline in the correct order. This game also features a game instruction screen, where you can find out more details about the pays. Instructional screens are available on all the IGT games in the series of video slot machines that I am showing you in this book.

I DREAM OF JEANNIE™

This new *I Dream of Jeannie*™ game is sure to grant your wishes for exciting spinning reel action in a delightfully whimsical theme that delivers perky pink nostalgia at the slightest command. On the game glass and top box, the vibrant pink, blond, and blue cartoons of television's favorite belly-dancing genie will attract fans of the show and supernatural skeptics alike. Brilliantly displayed symbols blaze on all five reels of this mystically enticing multi-coin game.

When you reel in one *I Dream of Jeannie*™ symbol this doubles the winning combinations as Jeannie (Barbara Eden) coos congratulations like "Are you pleased, master?" or "Is it not fun?" and "Ooh, master, you're a winner." As

the *I Dream of Jeannie*™ theme music issues from ear-level and subwoofer speakers, the enhanced digital stereo system accompanies all the jumpin' genie game action with sitcom-evoking sounds—Jeannie's folded arm "jajink," swirling pink bottle mist, a flying carpet swoop, and memorable Jeannie quips like "I am happy here with thee," and "How fortunate I am to have thee for a master." So put down that sitar and feel like a sultan, or a queen. To see what this game looks like, available in the upright version with the bonus wheel, see Photo 35.

35. Upright version of *I Dream of Jeannie*™ video slots, this one with the bonus spinning wheel at the top.

VIDEO MEGABUCKS®

This is the granddaddy of all multi-link progressives—the new *Video Megabucks*® machine from IGT.

This impressive *MegaJackpots*™ game takes the proven *Megabucks*® theme to a new level. The famous spinning reel game is now available in a 5-reel, 12-line video slot machine with two new bonus games. You will revel in the luxurious look and feel of the *Video Megabucks®* game. Twelve paylines provide more ways to win and exciting new bonus games will make you feel like a megawinner (see Photo 36).

There are several ways to gain extra wins through the bonus rounds. Three or more scattered Dollar Sign symbols launch the Pick A Buck bonus, which yields a value that is multiplied by the total bet. Three *Megabucks®* symbols on a played payline start the Mega-

36. The new *Video Megabucks®* wide area progressive video slot machine from IGT, in the slanttop style.

Match bonus. You will be asked to look for three matching symbols—money, limousines, jet planes, and more—and win the associated credits. This bonus game also includes a two-times and a five-times multiplier that can add up to 10 times the opulence to any jackpot. To see what these bonus screens look like, see Photos 37(a) through 37(d).

37(a). Pick a Buck Bonus screen.

The top jackpot, of course, happens when five of the recognizable *Megabucks®* Eagle symbols land on the twelfth payline with max coins bet. This then awards the *MegaJackpot*™! Too rich to be true, the *Video Megabucks®* game will add an air of

lavish sophistication to your winning portfolio. Look for this game in your favorite casino by the familiar *Megabucks*™ name and the fast-growing progressive meter.

37(b). Pick a Buck Win screen.

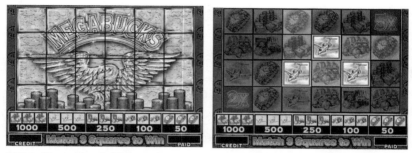

37(c). Mega Match Pick screen.   **37(d).** Mega Match Win screen.

THE PRICE IS RIGHT™

When a game becomes very popular, it is only natural that it evolves into different versions. This was the case with the two games I just showed you, and it is also the case with *The Price Is Right*™. This hugely popular game show has been on television for over 30 years, and the first versions of this video slot machine were such popular games that IGT came out with this new video slot version. Here's the newest version of the game in this new video slot machine, called *Punch a Bunch*™.

The Price Is Right™ Video Slots Featuring *Punch a Bunch™*

It's true that players love game themes based on popular television game shows and *The Price Is Right™* featuring *Punch a Bunch™* game is no exception. Based on the longest running game show in television history, this 15-line, 75-coin game is ready to invite you to "come on down"! *The Price Is Right™* featuring *Punch a Bunch™* game is configured as a nickel game, with multi-denominational capabilities (in approved jurisdictions). With bonus games you will recognize from the show, audience applause, interactive touchscreen action, and the enthusiastic voice of announcer Rod Roddy, this game recreates all the fun and excitement of the television game show experience. Distinguishing features of this popular game include a large vertical reel in the top box for attention-getting bonus game play, and an eye-catching topper with the show's highly identifiable logo and a static meter displaying the top award. The top award is paid when five *The Price Is Right™* symbols line up on the fifteenth payline with maximum credits wagered (see Photo 38).

38. *The Price Is Right™ Punch a Bunch™* video slots.

Punch a Bunch™ Bonus

The first of two bonuses, this one is triggered when three *Punch a Bunch™* symbols appear on reels one, two, and three, and this then initiates the *Punch a Bunch™* bonus game. You will be prompted to choose three of the five retail products from the table and are awarded the number of punches revealed by their choices. You then progress to a screen filled with balloons and are instructed by Roddy to "punch" the number of balloons you've earned. Punching (touching the video screen) a balloon reveals an amount (from 10 to 150 times the initiating line bet). If a "2nd Chance" balloon is revealed, you are instructed to choose additional balloons equal to the original number awarded. As Rod Roddy says, "Now that's a great bonus!"

Showcase Showdown™ Bonus

The second great bonus on this game happens when three or more *Showcase Showdown*™ symbols appear from left to right on a played line, and this then initiates the *Showcase Showdown*™ bonus game. You get to earn a chance to go to the showcase by spinning the big reel located in the top box. As in the television game show, you try to accumulate from 55 to 100 bonus credits in one or two spins, and win the total of your spins, plus advance to the showcase round. All credits accumulated during the Showcase Showdown bonus game are multiplied by the initiating bet for a really grand total. If the first spin or the sum of the two spins equals 100, the player is awarded an additional spin. If the

extra spin equals 100 exactly, 750 credits are awarded. Those who exceed 100 credits in the first round are awarded a consolation prize of 5 credits. When in the showcase round, you are asked to choose on-screen price tags until you've won

39(a). Showcase bonus screen.

all the credits assigned to one of the two showcases. Those who have picked all but two tags without winning a showcase are rewarded with the chance to win *both* showcases, and that becomes yet another great bonus. Take a look at all these bonus screens in Photos 39(a) through 39(c).

39(b). Wheel Spin screen.

39(c). Reels Wheel bonus screen.

This concludes my Top 10 list of the very best of the newest video slot machines and games. These are available in your favorite casino, and if they are not, ask the casino managers to get them. Of course, this doesn't mean that any of the other great video slots in the rest of this book are "chopped liver." This only means that I feel these first 10 machines and games are the most easily played for the fastest money value profits. The rest of the games I am about to show you are nothing to sneeze at either! All of these terrific games offer something special, and each has a specific value of its own. Some pay more on the base game, while others pay better on the bonus rounds. Some are more fun to play, while others are more profitable when played for longer periods of time. It all depends on what you are after, and whether your primary interest is in being entertained, or to win money. Although all these games offer both great entertainment value as well as money value, there are several distinct differences in each of these games that are well worth knowing about. A balance needs to be struck between entertainment and profitability, but a smart slot player knows that exploiting video slots for profits often requires more knowledge than just how to put the money in and how to push the button. The games themselves are intricate gambling devices, and just as it is important to learn to understand the cards in games like blackjack, so it is important to understand the machines, their pays, their symbols, what does what, how, when, how much it costs, what it offers, how many lines, how many bonuses, what you need to do to get to the bonus rounds, how much it is likely to cost you to get the bonuses, and so on—all of which are part of the skills of playing video slots, and skills in machine and game selection, as well as in how you approach each game and how you play it. Just because the machines look simple to play doesn't mean you have to immediately turn your brain off and blindly feed your money into the machine's coffers. Players who habitually lose money playing video slots seem to think that thinking isn't required and unfortunately, there are many video slots out there that may look like a good investment, but in reality are hungry games that eat your cash. If you really understand what the games are truly about, by reading this book and my other books as well, you will be well on your way toward understanding how to find the better games and how to play them for your benefit. Making powerful profits from video slots is not just the blind act of putting in the money, pushing the button, and hoping for the best. Blind luck will strike, but better luck is *calculated* luck based on *skills* and *knowledge*. And so, let us now move on to some of the other great video slots that are prime candidates for your gaming pleasure.

The 10 Most Fun
Video Slots

My list of favorite video slots is really a top 40 of the best casino video games now available. However, I wanted to divide them between those that I think are the all-time best—my Top 10 list in the previous chapter—and those that are, for instance, the most fun. At first, I thought it would be easy to separate these great games into categories, but it turned out not so. I wanted to include some of the games from this chapter, and from the chapters that follow, in the Top 10 list, and to include some of the top 10 in these later chapters.

Just because the machines and games in this chapter, and in the later chapters, are not specifically included in the Top 10 list does *not* mean that they are inferior to those in the Top 10 chapter. I am merely trying to separate these games into equal lots of 10 games per chapter. All the games and machines I have selected for this book fall smack into the best-of-the-best video slots around.

I have placed these games in separate chapters, each with its own particular heading to describe the 10 machines within each chapter. The 10 games in *this* chapter happen to be the most fun. While they are also good profit centers, offering solid money value for correct play, they have the added element of being really interesting and enjoyable to play. I begin with the game that just tickles me so much that I have to laugh out loud sometimes, especially when some of those zany bonuses hit. This is the *I Love Lucy*® video slot machine, this new one being part of the *MegaJack-pots*™ progressive family of video slots. I described an earlier version of this game, in my book *Powerful Profits from Slots*, so if you want to you can read up on that game, and then continue with me here as I describe the latest version of this very funny, and fun, video slot machine.

I LOVE LUCY® VIDEO SLOTS

Sweet things happen when you get into the act with the *I*

Love Lucy® game. This 12-line nickel game treats you to tasty bonus games, rewarding scatter pays, and original film clips. Stay tuned for sweet returns as Lucy, Ricky, Fred, and Ethel tickle everyone's funny bones in this highly entertaining game. The *I Love Lucy*® game is available in a *Mega-Jackpots*™ linked-progressive configuration or a stand-alone version (in jurisdictions where *MegaJackpots*™ linked-progressives are not available). A fixed or operator-configurable maximum bet feature is available for the stand-alone version (based on jurisdictional specifications). Whether you choose to play the upright or slant-top model, this highly recognizable game theme will, in true Lucy fashion, attract plenty of attention! (See Photo 40.)

40. *I Love Lucy*® video slot machine, this one with the Chocolate Factory theme.

Only Lucy could turn a boring chocolate factory job into one of the most hilarious sitcom episodes of all time! Line up three or more consecutive Lucy's Chocolate Factory bonus symbols (beginning with reel 1) on a played line and it's time for Lucy's Chocolate Factory bonus game. You will be coached by the floor matron to press the on-screen heart symbol to help Lucy fill the chocolate box. The excitement builds as the conveyor belt speed increases and the chocolates become more difficult to grab. Each piece of chocolate is assigned a credit value, and the faster the belt speed, the higher the values. Lucy's Chocolate Factory bonus game ends when Lucy fills the box and the player is awarded the combined credit value of the chocolates in the box.

The next bonus game happens when three or more Classic Moments symbols land in any position on the reels. This initiates the Classic Moments bonus game. Each Classic Moments symbol becomes a scene from an episode in the show's 10-year run. You will be asked to choose one of the symbols to activate the accompanying film clip and are awarded the number of credits revealed after the film clip ends.

In addition to the bonuses, line pays, and the progressive feature of this new game, the Ricky Ricardo's Club Babalu symbols function as scatter pay symbols. When three, four, or five symbols land in any position on the reels, you will win credits based on the total initiating bet and the number of symbols hit. Even more fun is the fact that the *I Love Lucy®*

41(a). Lucy's Chocolate Factory bonus screen.

41(b). Classic Moments bonus game screen.

heart symbols are wild and match any other symbol, except for the Lucy's Chocolate Factory, Classic Moments, or Ricky Ricardo's Club Babalu symbols. And, naturally, when you line up all five of the *I Love Lucy*® heart symbols across the twelfth payline with max credits wagered, you will win the top jackpot. The progressive jackpot (as part of a linked progressive system) is paid in a single installment upon verification of win. You can see these bonus screens in Photos 41(a) and 41(b).

And just to make sure there's even more fun for you, when you touch any of the character faces between game play you will hear original sound clips from the show, from Ricky's "Luuuucy!" to Lucy's "Waaaaaaah!" Now that's a fun game, indeed!

HARLEY-DAVIDSON® VIDEO SLOTS

There's nothing sweet about this video slot machine game, but that doesn't mean it isn't fun. As I've hinted in my earlier Slots book, this is a rumble of a good time. This new version of the game has added penny denomination to the game play, still based on the popular appeal of Harley-Davidson® motorcycles. This is a 5-reel, 15-line, 150-coin game that features a top-box bonus full of high-energy excitement. Photo 42 shows this new version.

There are two of these high-energy bonuses: the Eagle bonus, where you select from three, four, or five Eagle symbols anywhere on the reels, and the Road Rally bonus that features several rounds of interactive game play focusing on the top-box reel. The Road Rally bonus can also trigger the Great American Rally bonus, which adds extra credits to the bonus win.

The top jackpot happens when five *Harley-Davidson®* jackpot symbols land on the first payline, with a maximum bet on all paylines. This will pay the progressive jackpot, where available by gaming jurisdiction, or a fixed jackpot amount depending on what is available at the casino where you are playing. In some casinos, this

42. The rumblin' new version of the *Harley-Davidson®* video slot machine.

non-progressive top jackpot will also win you a real Harley-Davidson® motorcycle, so be sure to bring your leather jacket and helmet when you play this game.

LIFESTYLES OF THE RICH AND FAMOUS® VIDEO SLOTS

As the perfect segue for the high-rolling action of the *Harley-Davidson®* game, we are now going to ride straight into the world of champagne wishes and caviar dreams, which can mean—of course—only one thing: The *Lifestyles of the Rich and Famous®*, along with the host with the most, Robin Leach. You deserve to live the high life with this brand new video slot machine. This 15-line, 75-coin video slot may also be available as a *MegaJackpots™* linked-progressive game (*MegaJackpots™* top award paid in installments upon verification of win), or a stand-alone progressive model where *MegaJackpots™* games are not available. With the power of the new AVP processor, vivid colors, stunning animation, and enhanced stereo sound, the *Lifestyles of the Rich and Famous®* game certainly does give you that rich feeling.

The *Lifestyles of the Rich and Famous®* video slot comes in an amazing new package, starting with the eye-catching modern cabinet. That is the new *Game King Royal* 19-inch upright model that features a new cabinet styling, an ergonomic button panel, bright topper artwork, and a backlit monitor mask. But the exterior packaging is just the beginning. The new monitor provides a clearer picture and brighter colors, which means players can see the animation in all its glory. The enhanced graphics and exciting game play combine for a luxurious gaming experience. Limo, mansion, and yacht symbols animate in amazing 3-D fashion when they land in winning combinations, adding extra adrenaline to the thrill of receiving a big payout. You can see this game in Photo 43.

The *Lifestyles of the Rich and Famous®* bonus envelops you in a sumptuous atmosphere. Robin Leach welcomes you to the bonus, and the screen provides instructions for game play. You get to select one tile from each row on the 4-row, 5-column grid, which then animates to reveal luxury items and their associated credit value. When all of the selections are made, you can accept the total credit offered, or try again. If you choose to try again, you can change any selection on any row, up to three selections. The game displays the credits associated with both the old and the new selection, giving you

43. *Lifestyles of the Rich and Famous®* video slot machine.

44(a). Robin Leach introduces the bonus.

a chance to see if your choice improves the win. Play continues until the number of changes left is zero, you accept an offer, or you uncover the items worth the highest credit value. You can see these bonus game screens in Photos 44(a) through 44(c).

Naturally, the top reel award is triggered when five *Lifestyles of the Rich and Famous*® symbols land on payline 15 with a maximum wager. This is sure to place you firmly in the company of the rich and famous.

44(b). Bonus Pick screen.

AUSTIN POWERS™— INTERNATIONAL GAME OF MYSTERY™

Get ready for a British invasion like you've never seen before! It's *Austin Powers™— International Game of Mystery™*! Swingin' London will have nothing on your

44(c). Bonus conclusion screen.

floor, baby, once you get a load of this groovy game that puts the GRRR in gaming. Yes, that's right . . . shagadelic super-spy *Austin Powers™* is at it again . . . saving the world from *Dr.*

Evil™ and his wicked cohorts. During five mojo-boosting bonus bouts, players are transported back to the day when discotheques ruled the scene and go-go boots were high fashion. Zany clips from Austin's movies will keep you in stitches as *Frau Farbissina*™ keeps the game moving by shrieking high-pitched commands in her notorious German accent. And, to make things even more exciting, the cast of the bonus scenes keeps changing—you will never have the same gaming experience twice! Jam-packed with excitement, this game comes in a totally decked out package that features three different glass themes and a "Groovy Baby!" topper. After playing this smashing game, you'll be shouting, "Yeah, baby, yeah!"

This very hip game comes in two models, the 17-inch upright round top, 10-inch, or 16-inch top box, and the 19-inch slant-top with the arch or the 13-inch top box. The "Groovy Baby" topper, with its mesmerizing flower-power background, comes in either a chrome or a gold finish and is complemented by three different glass themes: *Austin Powers*™ himself, his nemesis *Dr. Evil*™ with Mini Me™, and Austin's lovely comrades-in-arms, *Felicity Shagwell*™ and *Vanessa Kensington*™.

45. *Austin Powers*™ *International Game of Mystery*™ video slots.

Take a look at this stunning game in Photo 45, and you will notice that this is a new design, different in many of its features from the one I introduced in my earlier Slots book. What makes this game even more different is a variation called The Time Portal, which I will show you in just a moment. First, let's take a look at the various bonuses available in this version of the *Austin Powers*™ video slot machine.

The Fembot bonus round initiates when three *Frau Farbissina*™ symbols land on any payline. *Frau Farbissina*™ yells, "Bring in the Fembots!" and at the Pick a Fembot bonus screen the game prompts you to pick a fembot. When you choose either the left or the right fembot, the chosen vixen uses her machine-gun bra to shoot out the pattern of the bonus into the air. When you choose the middle fembot, she uses her gas-emitting bra to release a pink cloud that, once it clears, reveals the bonus.

The Faces of Austin bonus round initiates when three or more *Austin Powers*™ symbols land on any payline. Swanky bonus round music begins and the Austin symbols are highlighted. When you select an Austin, the symbol launches into a video clip from one of the movies. Once the clip is finished, the game displays the bonus.

The Henchman bonus round initiates when three *Dr. Evil*™ symbols land on any payline. *Dr. Evil*™ menacingly sneers "Ladies and Gentlemen, welcome to my underground lair," and, at the Eliminate a Henchman bonus screen, the game prompts you to "Replace Credits with Multiplier." When you select a henchman, the evil menace falls back into a pit of flames, and the henchman's bonus value is displayed. This value is then crossed out and a multiplier is displayed. Once all the multipliers have been selected and added together, *Frau Farbissina*™ yells, "End of bonus!" and the game reveals the remaining henchmens' credit values. These credit values are then added up, multiplied by the final multiplier, and added to the credit meter.

The Match bonus round initiates when five symbols of either *Felicity Shagwell*™ or *Vanessa Kensington*™ land on any payline. At the Select and Match bonus screen, the game prompts you to select symbols. When a symbol is selected, a character appears and says a line from one of the Austin movies. When a match is made, it's highlighted on the Match Win scoreboard. If you select the *Fat Bastard*™ symbol, *Frau Farbissina*™ notifies you that you can make only one more match and then the bonus round ends. If you find the Mojo symbol during the Match bonus, all awards are doubled.

Austin Powers™ Time Portal

This is the newest version of this game, and is "Groovy Baby! Yeah!" You'll swoon at the sight of this addition to the series of sexy themes that are part of these new video slots. Shagadelic game play and big jackpots will keep you spellbound. Do you love the game? Yeah Baby! Yeah! This game invites you to take a trip back to the days when bell bottoms and hot pants were the swinging new fashions. Based on the hit movies, this game features psychedelic reel symbols, cool music, and entertaining game play with a mesmerizing twist (see Photo 46).

46. *Austin Powers*™ *Time Portal* video slot machine.

In addition to the bonuses, this game also pays a scatter pay that will make you "behave" when two, three, four, or five *Austin Powers*™ *Time Portal* symbols land anywhere on the reels. The *Austin Powers*™ symbol is wild, and substitutes for all other symbols except the *Time Portal* symbol. You'll shimmy with delight when you see the double payout that results.

47(a). *Time Portal* bonus screen 15 free games.

The *Time Portal* bonus launches you to a richer time and place when three or more *Time Portal* symbols land anywhere on the reels. You receive a scatter pay and 15 free spins. The reels move hypnotically during each spin, and when they land, all winning payouts are tripled. You're in for more time-traveling fun when three or more *Time Portal* symbols land during bonus game play, triggering another 15 free games. To see the bonus screens, check out Photos 47(a) and 47(b).

When five *Austin Powers*™ symbols land on an active payline with a maximum bet, the game pays a top jackpot, worthy of a shout of "Yeah Baby! Yeah!" Mod music, hippie-inspired reel symbols and swinging game play will make you shake

47(b). Bonus Spin Reels screen.

in your go-go boots. Any '60s hipster would agree that the *Austin Powers*™ *Time Portal* video slot is one shagadelic gaming experience.

SERIES *AUSTIN POWERS*™ IN *GOLDMEMBER*™ VIDEO SLOTS

Not to be outdone, there is yet another version of this game, based on the newest installment in the movie series, *Goldmember*. Travel back to 1975 when roller disco ruled the

48. *Austin Powers™ Goldmember™* video slots.

nightlife and get down with the platform shoes and polyester stylings of *Austin Powers™* in *Goldmember™*! This 5-reel, 15-line, 75-coin game features the disco-loving Goldmember as well as a groovy cast of characters. (See Photo 48.)

In addition to the now traditional features for the *Austin Powers™* video slots series, this version offers two bonuses. The Disco Spin bonus starts when one on-screen she-spy reveals the number of disco ball spins. Touch the on-screen disco ball to start spinning the top box disco ball and you will win the value of the section where the ball stops, times the initiating line bet. If you land on an Extra Spin section, this will award the same number of spins as initially hit, in addition to those already obtained.

The Mini-Movie bonus starts when you are prompted to select an Austin symbol, where you will win from one to six mini-movie selections. Pick a selection to view a memorable movie moment, which will award you a win from 3 to 24 credits, times the total initiating bet. If you also receive the Bonus Pick Plus symbol, you win the value of the symbol as well as an additional selection.

The top jackpot is paid when five *Austin Powers™* in *Goldmember™* symbols appear on the fifteenth line with maximum bet wagered. This pays the *Classic Comedy Mega-Jackpots™* top award (paid instantly upon verification of win). Linked-progressive jackpots are not available in all gaming jurisdictions, and in those cases stand-alone games are available in areas where progressives are not. On those games, the top jackpot will be a fixed amount, so check the pay table for details.

UNO® VIDEO SLOTS

With the highly recognizable symbols of the classic card game populating the video reels, this 5-reel, 15-line, 75-coin nickel game provides you with a deck full of video excitement. America's favorite card game is now a video slot! Available as a nickel game, this version of the machine is also a progressive, where available. In addition to the traditional pays, this game also offers a scatter pay and two bonuses. (See Photo 49.)

49. *UNO*® video slot machine from IGT.

Triple UNO® Bonus

You can discard as many cards as possible in three rounds, and each discarded card earns you additional credits.

UNO® *ATTACK*® Scatter Pay

This feature is triggered by three or more *UNO*® *ATTACK*® symbols, and pays up to 7,500 credits per scatter pay. These are paid in addition to line and bonus wins.

Double Up Feature

In some casinos this game also offers you the chance for double-or-nothing option, after winning combinations have been determined. Check the machine's pay table and bonus screens for details before you start playing to find out if the game in your casino offers this version. There are many casinos around the United States, and around the world, where such options may not be allowed under the various gaming regulations, but it is easy to find this out just by looking at the game's own instructional and pay table screens.

Top Jackpot

The top jackpot is paid when five *UNO®* symbols land on the fifteenth line with maximum bet wagered. This will be a progressive, where *MegaJackpots*™ linked-progressives are available.

SALE OF THE CENTURY

50. *Sale of the Century* video slot machine.

One of the '70s most exciting game shows, this *Sale of the Century* 5-reel, 9-line, 45-credit nickel video slot game features the fabulous prize symbols that made it a television hit, including the animated hawker Joe Garagiola to guide you through game play. Available as a stand-alone version or on a *MegaJackpots*™ linked-progressive as a member of the Game Show Greats lineup, the *Sale of the Century* game is a sure-fire winner. (See Photo 50.)

Only a thin purple line divides you from a big win if three Wall of Fame symbols land on reels one, two, and three of a played line. Following Joe's instructions, you are asked to select three character squares from the grid of familiar faces to reveal credit rewards and additional bonus plays. If one of the chosen squares reveals purple highlights, the multiplier increments as you advance to another Wall of Fame to select three more characters. Continue to select three characters from each new Fame Wall until none of the selected squares is highlighted and the bonus pays the revealed credits times the accumulated multiplier.

You'll be transported to center stage for the choice of a lifetime in the Free Spins bonus, when three or more animated Joe symbols land anywhere on the reels. Follow Joe's instructions and choose a button—the better choice is green for optimal play. If red is chosen the number of free spins is reeled in and the win increased by the multiplier to end the bonus round. Select green to take a chance on increasing the number of free spins and the multiplier value awarded

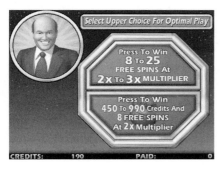

by picking one of the fabulous showroom prizes, but please note that the merchandise is for display only and is not awarded. Once the number of spins and the new multiplier is revealed, a set of special reels round up your reward. Additional spins may be awarded during the bonus

51(a). Bonus Decision screen.

with three or more animated Joe symbols in any position. The bonus ends when the free spin meter reaches zero or after a whopping 990 free spins have been won and played. You can see these bonus screens in Photos 51(a) through 51(d).

Sale of the Century logo symbols go wild with merchandise and playing card

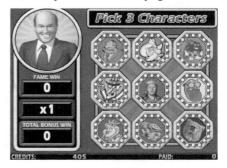

51(b). Wall of Fame bonus screen.

51(c). Pick a Prize screen.

symbols. Line up five *Sale of the Century* symbols on a payline with the maximum bet wagered and take home the top award! You'll win either an Instant Winners linked-progressive *MegaJackpots™* jackpot on the Game Show Greats network or a set amount in jurisdictions where *MegaJackpots™* are not available. Relive the era of wide ties and even wilder game show action with *EZ Pay™ Sale of the Century* video slots, because "take it or leave it, I'm still Joe Garagiola." Well, I'm not really Joe, but they do call me "Vegas Vic," so I guess that's close.

51(d). Free Spin Reels screen.

BEETLE BAILEY'S® ONE-DAY PASS OUT VIDEO SLOTS

At ease, troops! You are relieved to join the comical cadre from Camp Swampy for some well-deserved R & R with the *Beetle Bailey's® One-Day Pass Out* video slots—a 25-line, 125-coin game featuring classic anecdotes from America's favorite comic strip, and the Andrews Sisters' jazzy, fanfare favorite—"Boogie Woogie Bugle Boy." So hop outta that foxhole and hit the deck running—you are "Diiiiiiiiiiismissed!" (See Photo 52.)

Every soldier knows there's only one way to really resolve a one-day pass. Beer Bust! Hoah! Round up three

Mug-of-Beer bonus symbols on the first, second, and third reels of a played line and you're in for some hilarious drinking game fun in the *One-Day Pass Out* bonus. In this bonus game, your objective is to choose a soldier and hope he stays on his feet as the libations flow because every mug of beer slung to the thirsty patrons pays bonus credits until one of the characters passes out. If your chosen character stands his ground, you progress to the next round. You may choose to stick with your favorite patron in each successive round or pick another; either way, in each round progressively higher credit awards are paid for each drink consumed. If any character begins to teeter, only a reviving kiss by the curvaceous Miss Buxley will continue the round . . . and, if your stout-hearted imbiber is the last man standing, you receive the house special and an extra award to end the bonus game.

52. *Beetle Bailey®* video slot machine.

Classic Sarge versus Beetle action takes place in the Beetle Bop bonus, which is triggered when three Beetle Bop symbols line up across reels two, three, and four. As the base game symbols fade, the three bonus symbols transform into a double-talking Beetle Bailey sandwiched by two glowering Sgt Snorkels. Select one of the three highlighted character symbols to view an animated comic clip and receive a bonus credit award.

Flag-waving *Beetle Bailey®* symbols are wild with the animated comic strip characters and their military equipment, or pay a scatter bonus when three or more of the patriotic logo symbols land on the reels. Capture five *Beetle Bailey®* symbols anywhere on the reels and no matter what lines are played, not even a Sgt Snorkel–sized foxhole will hold your Rapid Hit Progressive jackpot award! Stuffed with an eye-catching panoply of Beetle Bailey® comic characters and capped with an optional distortion art topper and progressive meter, the *Beetle Bailey® One-Day Pass Out* video slot game will have you yellin' Hoah! and dancing a "beer polka" jig.

18 REELER™ VIDEO SLOTS

You will make the long haul to have some good truckin' fun when you get your hands on the *18 Reeler*™ game, a mon-

ster theme with a towering top box that drives the bold sensations of the open road right onto the casino floor. Eighteen reels yield 40 possible paylines, and a truckload of fun and visual action with every spin! This game features an eye-catching top box and also incorporates the top box into game play for more exciting ways to win. To see this game, here's Photo 53.

Watch out! Because after the scatter pays hit you head-on, you'll need to pull in at the nearest truck stop to clean all those bonus credits off your wind-

53. *18 Reeler*™ video slot machine.

shield. Scatter pays award from 3 to 250 times the total bet. If five trucker symbols land on a played line, you can win up to 700 times the initiating bet and you get to play the Big Haul bonus. If five *18 Reeler*™ symbols land on a played line, you win 10,000 times the initiating bet! Come back? That's affirmative, and a big 10-4, good buddy—10,000 times and you get to go to the bonus round!

Now get ready for a road trip. You'll feel as if you're right behind the wheel and in control of the road in the Big Haul bonus. During this bonus, the grid of credit values on the grille of the towering, truck-like top box comes into play. You'll be caught in the headlights while the game randomly selects values from squares on the grid and multiplies them by the line bet. After two rounds of selecting squares, you'll really start to fill the credit tank up when you get the bonus awards up to 1,000 additional credits! For example, on the third round, you get the credit value on the truck grille plus five. If you've got enough motion lotion (that's gasoline to you four-wheelers) to go five rounds without landing on a duplicate credit value, make way for another 25. And that's just the beginning. If you roll through nine rounds without landing on a duplicate credit value, you're outta there with 1,000 more credits! The credits accumulate and the bonus shifts into high gear until a duplicate square is found or until nine squares are selected.

Does the fun and winning ever stop? You never know who you'll run into at the end of the road. Aliens? A magic bus? The cops? You'll laugh out loud at the comical surprise endings to the bonus action. Stereo sounds surround the action, featuring amusing CB chatter, air horn blasts, and familiar theme music. When you see this game—and it's impossible to miss—you'll know players will drop the hammer and put the pedal to the metal to play this video slot. Keep your eyes out for the bears, we'll catch ya on the flip side.

DOUBLE DIAMOND® FAST-HIT™ PROGRESSIVE VIDEO SLOTS

The *Double Diamond®* spinning reel game has long been a player favorite. To make a good game better, IGT engineers and game developers created the innovative *Double Diamond®*

iGame-Plus™ video slot, with a progressive jackpot. This is a frequently hitting progressive jackpot, with the base game being a 5-reel, 9-line, 27-credit max bet *Double Diamond®* *Fast-Hit*™ Progressive. To view this game, see Photo 54.

Because I have already described the *Double Diamond®* and "double pay" machines in my earlier book, *Powerful Profits from Slots*, I will now briefly list the new features that can be found in this video game.

Game Features of the *New Double Diamond® Fast-Hit*™ Progressive Video Slot Machine

- Five-reel, nine-line video slot theme
- 27-credit max bet Multi-Denomination game
- Familiar *Double Diamond®* multiplier-style play
- Frequent progressive hits about every 15,000 games
- Fabulous gems, shiny gold, and sparkling jewelry fill every reel spin

  - *Double Diamond®* symbols only appear on reels two, three, or four
  - *Double Diamond®* symbols match winning symbol combinations appearing on consecutive reels of a played line from the far left—except the *Fast-Hit*™ symbol
  - Matching *Double Diamond®* symbols multiply winning symbol combination awards
  - Match one *Double Diamond®* symbol to double award
  - Two symbols multiply award 4 times
  - Three symbols awards 8 times the winning combination
  - Spinning up three or four animated *Fast-Hit*™ symbols to any position on

54. *Double Diamond®* video slot machine with a 100,000-coin top jackpot.

the reels, for any number of played lines, pays a
spectacular scatter award in addition to payline
wins

- Landing five *Fast-Hit*™ symbols anywhere on the
  reels, with max bet, pays the progressive meter
  award upon verification

As with all of the games in this chapter, the *Double
Diamond*® machines are not only great fun, but also good
payers. This has always been so for the reel version of this
game, and the video version doesn't disappoint either.
Together, the machines and games in this chapter follow
from those I presented in the earlier chapter, and are now
followed by the next crop of video slot machines—those I
have grouped among what I call the "best bonuses." However, as I mentioned earlier, just because the games in the
next chapter are placed under this best bonuses category,
doesn't mean that the other machines and games in this
book aren't as good. It simply means that I have decided to
separate all these great games into different chapters according to their best features. Okay, let's see what's up in
the next batch of the greatest video slots now available in
any casino, anywhere.

The 10 Best Bonuses in Video Slots

There used to be a time when slot machine manufacturers would shy away from anything that would disturb the established principles of slot play. At that time the reasoning was that players would be confused if there were too many things to do on the slot machine. Players of the era of the mechanical and electromechanical slot machines liked the simplicity of the game—put in a coin, pull the handle, see what you win. Of course the old mechanical machines could not be configured to pay bonuses, certainly none like we know today. When the electromechanical machines came to be, they offered many more jackpots and larger pay amounts, and although some were capable of being configured for a bonus-like payoff, that persistent reasoning that said KISS— or "kiss," meaning "keep it simple stupid"—prevented much other innovation from happening. It wasn't until the advances in computer technology permitted increased processor capacity and memory that slot manufacturers began to again consider improving the traditional slot machines.

Although this resulted in some of the first "themed" reel machines, what we now consider as "bonusing" really didn't start happening until the mid-1990s. Four important factors in the successful development of slot machine bonusing had to converge at about the same time.

- First, there had to be the technological capability, which by that time existed in the form of higher processor speeds for the computers that ran the games along with the increased memory capacity required to make this work.
- Second, the gaming innovators had to be there, and had to have the ideas and foresight to imagine the possibilities. This came in the form of the video-arcade generation of game innovators.

Men like IGT's Joe Kaminkow, who is the genius behind most of the great games you see in this book, took their skill in developing arcade-style video games and transferred this into the development of gambling video games, and the video slot machine was born with full force. These innovators also considered that the players would like to have "something more." An event, or a series of events, that would be earned through play would transport the player into another dimension of the base game, and offer them something extra, where they already know they are a winner. It was simply a killer concept. Who wouldn't like it? After all, once you hit the bonus round you know you have won already, and the question therefore is not "if" you will win, but simply "How much?" This was the beginning of the new generation of the twenty-first century video slots that you are now seeing in this book.

- The third important factor was customer acceptance.

The older generations didn't like the video slots because they liked the simplicity of the mindless coin-in-and-pull-the-handle reel slot machine that looked like the old mechanical clunkers, even though by that time these were just as computerized as any of the video slots. That didn't matter, because as long as the machines looked like and felt like the old handle-pullers, the players felt comfortable with them. The video slot machine had to wait also for the casino players to catch up to the technology by their acceptance. This had to wait for the arcade kids to grow up and become not only players in casinos, but also managers, employees, and casino executives.

- The final major item was the convergence of the innovation, the technology, the player's acceptance of the new machines, and the casino executive's willingness to allocate casino floor space to the new machines.

When all four of these key situations merged, we saw the explosion of video slots transform the casinos of the twentieth century into the modern video casinos of the twenty-first century. At about 1985, the casinos still derived more than 70 percent of their revenue from gambling table games. By 2003, more than 80 percent of all casino gaming revenue comes from slots, and of this more than two-thirds come from video slots. Soon there will be more and more video slots on the casino floor and, eventually, there will be holographic gaming stations where the patrons enter the virtual world and will be offered any kind of casino game they wish, in any virtual world environment they care to experience. Sounds like sci-fi? Well, it's already here. As machines become coinless, then cashless, and technology surpasses even our own conception at this time, the same technology that now allows us to have holographic credit cards and money will very soon allow us entry into virtual worlds of video gambling. But, there is still time for us to sit back and enjoy the great video games we have in the casinos of today, and among those are the following that I like mostly for their bonuses.

SPAM® VIDEO SLOTS

SPAM®, the world's most famous canned meat, is served up in a 5-reel, 25-line *iGame-Plus*™ nickel machine that celebrates this most American of delicacies. From Traditional to Smoke Flavored, Lite to Roasted Turkey, you will line up for helping after helping of this tasty game. Animated reel symbols and snappy background music add '50s flair to the fun. When "*Spam*®–tacular" wordplay symbols or the wholesome characters—who suggest ways to prepare the versatile meat—connect in winning combinations, your mouth will be watering with anticipation. Animated dancing Spammy

cans trigger scatter pays when three or more land anywhere on the reels. Check out this game in Photo 55.

Two delicious bonus rounds will whet your appetite for another helping. The Rings of *SPAM*® bonus starts when three *SPAM*® Bonus Cookbook symbols land on the second, third, and fourth reels of an active payline. You will move through four concentric circles by selecting cans of *SPAM*® that

55. The brand new *SPAM*® video slot machine.

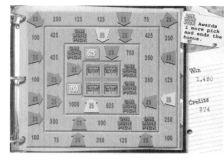

56(a). Rings of *SPAM®* bonus screen.

reveal bonus credits. If you uncover a One More Pick icon, the bonus ends after the next selection. When you find an arrow symbol, the bonus moves into the next ring, where higher credit values and more One More Pick icons are on the table. Players who make it all the way to the innermost ring receive one final selection worth extra bonus credits.

You will lick your chops when three or more USDA Grade A bonus symbols land anywhere on the reels, triggering the *SPAM®* Cook Off bonus. The game prompts you to pick one of three cans, which is transformed into festive all-American party food—such as a *SPAM®* football for a tailgate party or a lovable heart-shaped

56(b). Pick a Can of *SPAM®* Cook Off bonus screen.

56(c). *SPAM®* Cook Off final award bonus screen.

SPAM® for Valentine's Day. The delectable concoction is awarded a first-, second-, or third-place ribbon with the lucky player winning the associated prize value. You can see these bonus screens in Photos 56(a) through 56(c).

When you see that familiar *SPAM®* can topping this

Spamazing game, get your chops a lickin' 'cause this game's gonna keep you cookin'!

THE TERMINATOR™ VIDEO SLOTS

When actor Arnold Schwarzenegger was elected governor of the State of California in 2003, everyone immediately dubbed him the Governator. This is because he became most popular and known worldwide as the Terminator machine in the three films of that genre. As is the case with

most pop-culture phenomena, it was inevitable that *The Terminator* should become a video slot machine. "This is one *killer* game!," and that's exactly what you will be saying when you see *The Terminator*™ game. (See Photo 57.)

Towering menacingly above the casino floor, the life-size endoskeleton head of Skynet's Terminator scans the terrain searching for its next mark. All the while, action scenes from the movie, set to the notorious pulsating

57. *The Terminator*™ video slot machine from IGT.

58(a). Red Eye bonus screen.

Terminator theme, entice you to take a closer look. Once attracted to the game, you are thrust into your favorite movie roles during exceptional bonus round action. In the Red Eye bonus, you will get to use the Terminator's scanning grid to zoom and focus in on bonus credits. During the Hunter-Killer bonus, you engage in an all-out bonus-credit shooting war against another Terminator. And in Crush the Terminator, you launch bonus-credit laden weapons at an advancing Terminator. Photos 58(a) through 58(c) show these bonus screens.

After playing this game, you will not hesitate to say "I'll be back!" Just try not to mimic Arnold, unless, that is, you are really good at it, in which case it will sound funny.

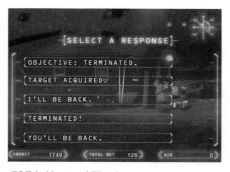

58(b). Hunter-Killer bonus screen.

58(c). Crush the Terminator screen.

ENCHANTED UNICORN®
VIDEO SLOTS

Let the princes, damsels, mushrooms, rasp-
berries, roses, of the *Enchanted Unicorn*®
video reel game transport you to a mythi-
cal kingdom. This 20-line *iGame-Plus*™
fairy tale features Celtic-inspired reel symbols for a truly ethereal gaming experience. The Unicorn symbol is wild: when
it lands anywhere on the second, third, or
fourth reels, its bonus is triggered. All winning symbol combinations are paid, then
all three reel symbols in the column magi-
cally transform into wild Unicorn sym-

59. *Enchanted
Unicorn*® video
slot machine.

60(a). Select a Tile bonus screen.

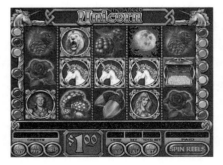

60(b). Treasure Chest bonus screen.

bols, which substitute for
all reel symbols but the
Treasure Chest. When that
symbol lands on the first
and fifth reels of a row, the
enchanting Treasure Chest
bonus begins. You will be
prompted to navigate through
a five-row, six-column grid
with one pick per row, searching for charmed credit values. If the mystical Unicorn
appears, you will receive
all the credit values for the
row. The game awards a
dreamlike bonus if you can
avoid the nasty werewolf. If
he rears his ugly head, the
bonus ends. See this game
and its bonus screens in
Photos 59, 60(a), and 60(b).

KENNY ROGERS® THE GAMBLER® VIDEO SLOTS

Famed singer Kenny Rogers probably couldn't have imagined that his song "The Gambler" would spawn several movies, and now a video slot machine. Now you can treat yourself to one of the best-known names in crowd-pleasing entertainment, with the *Kenny Rogers® The Gambler®* game. This 5-reel, 15-line game can be found with up to 20 credits per line—300 credits per spin—for a top award of 200,000 credits. (See Photo 61.)

I will now briefly explain some of the features of this great game, and show you the bonus screens in Photos 62(a) and 62(b).

61. *Kenny Rogers®* as *The Gambler®* video slot machine.

The Gambler® Video Slot Machine Game and Its Bonuses

- Two or more *Kenny Rogers®* picture scatter symbols anywhere on the reels multiply the total bet by two, five, or 20 times.
- Three Gambler bonus symbols in any position on the middle reels initiate *The Gambler®* bonus. Picking a poker chip reveals the number of hands that you will be offered in this hold 'em or fold 'em game. Features great music and animation.
- Any combination of five *Kenny Rogers®* logo and Free Spin Express symbols gets the Free Spin Express bonus chuggin' on down the track. You will be asked

62(a). *The Gambler* bonus screen.   **62(b).** Free Spin Express bonus

to pick boxcars to get free spins and multipliers. Each free spin places the initiating bet on all 15 lines.

THE FROG PRINCE® VIDEO SLOTS

This game is part of the IGT enchanted games series, like the *Enchanted Unicorn*® (discussed earlier). I like this particular game because it reminds me of my childhood stories

of noble princes and beautiful princesses, and even the frogs that turned to princes who got the girl and lived happily ever after. It is this kind of fantasy that inspires these video slots, and the theme doesn't disappoint. It is a storybook design, offering a 5-reel 15-line video slot game with great graphics and terrific sound effects, as well as animation and bonuses. There are castles, crowns, lively croaking frogs, and a host of other enchanted features that build a game mystique, including moon and star symbols that act as scatter pays. (See Photo 63.)

63. *The Frog Prince*® video slot machine.

There are two more great bonuses with

this game. In the Magic Wish bonus, you will be asked to pick one magic book to reveal the number of free bonus spins. Then you will get to select a magic wand, and in a

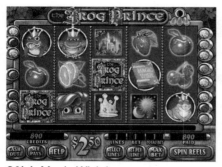

swirl of pixie dust the wand will reveal the multiplier for your credits during the free spins. You will be assured of a winner no matter what, and this adds the extra excitement to this bonus.

64(a). Magic Wish bonus screen.

The second bonus happens when three animated frogs land on the middle three reels. This is perhaps the most fun bonus of them all, because these frogs all have personalities and they don't mind letting you know it. Ribbitt! This takes you to the Kiss the Frog bonus, and the three optimistic frogs will all try to get you to pick them, hopeful that they will turn into a prince. If the frog turns into the Prince, you will get the top bonus award—but the frogs can also turn into a variety of other comical characters, six in all, each with its own personality and a purse of prize money. You get to choose if you want to keep that prize money, or kiss the frog again. You get to kiss the frog anywhere from three to five times, each time getting a different character with a different award. Of course the best strategy is always to pick again, because your goal is to pick the frog that turns into a prince, which

64(b). Kiss the Frog bonus screen.

wins you all the money. Photos 64(a) and 64(b) depict these bonus screens.

Of course you don't actually kiss the frogs—just touch the screen over the frog you pick—so don't worry about getting any warts. You won't get warts with this game, just awards (ugh, what a pun!).

MONEY STORM® VIDEO SLOTS

This video slot game will have you singing in the rain with its downpour of winning credits and wind-worried farm animal symbols that add comic relief to every reel spin. The Weather Beacon and Storm bonus rounds featured in this 5-reel, 20-line game offer you laugh-out-loud fun and winning excitement as it showers you with bonus credits. (See Photo 65.)

When three Weather Beacon symbols land in the same position on reels three, four, and five, the bonus round signals that a wave of bonus credits is about to rain down into your pockets! Watch as a whirlwind of bonus credits accumulate on the weather beacon. After this shower of credits is over, you will have won from 2 to 25 credits times the initiating wager.

When three or more *Money Storm*® bonus symbols land consecutively on a played line, you catch a cloudburst of credits as free scatter pay–spins automatically begin. You will laugh out loud at the animated symbols in this fury of fun. During this bonus round, credits are awarded for symbols falling anywhere on the reels. The game also offers the oppor-

65. *Money Storm*®

66(a). Weather Beacon Bonus screen.

tunity for "bonus within a bonus" game play action. If three Weather Beacon symbols land in the same position on reels three, four, and five, the bonus automatically starts awarding credits. If three *Money Storm*® bonus symbols land consecutively, the Storm scatter free spin bonus starts all over again! The bonus ends when zero free spins remain or after up to 200 free spins are complete. Photos 66(a) and 66(b) show these bonus screens.

It's a money storm, and a big one too! Let the *Money Storm*® video slot game add a downpour of fun to your gaming profits—it's sure to blow you away.

66(b). The *Money Storm*® bonus screen.

TABASCO®

Hot! Hot! Hot! That's the best way to describe *TABASCO*®, a spicy 5-reel, 9-line game for the *iGame-Plus*™ platform, where popular pepper sauces from Tasty to Atomic flavor game play. Mild but hot, this popular hot sauce will add saucy excitement to your casino gaming—just have plenty of water ready to put out the flames. With pepper sauces from the tasty Garlic to atomic Habanero coupled with the moving bass of a ferocious Zydeco beat spicing up the game, you will be grooving Cajun-style. You can see this spicy game in Photo 67.

The bonuses start when three or more of the *TABASCO*® Country Store symbols land on a played payline. This takes you to the Country Store bonus round, where products appear in a grid of squares. Uncover three different pepper sauce–logoed items and the matched crafts credit values are totaled for the bonus award.

The second bonus is the Kitchen with Claude bonus round, which showcases the versatility of the *TABASCO*® brand. You launch yourself into Claude's kitchen when you get the three Cajun Chef symbols lined up across reels two,

67. *TABASCO*®
video slot machine.

three, and four. As the base game symbols fade, the two outside Chefs—Squeegee and Luiggi—hoe-down as the center Chef symbol spins out tasty ingredients for the four *TABASCO*®-influenced recipe favorites lining the top of the screen. When you gather three unique ingredients to complete a delta-seasoned dish, Chef Claude whips up your tasty bonus award.

The third bonus happens when flavored fans and catchy Cajun music attract three or more mosquitoes anywhere on the reels, causing these sucker slappers to pay you more credits. This is a funny and great-paying scatter feature.

The fourth bonus is really more of a game content bonus, because the *TABASCO*® symbols act as "wild," substituting for the other animated symbols of the base game screen. When all five of these diamond-shaped *TABASCO*® symbols line up on a played payline, then you win the top

68(a). Country Store bonus screen.   **68(b).** Kitchen with Claude bonus screen.

jackpot. See these bonus screens in Photos 68(a) through 68(c).

There are other versions of this game also available, where three or more *PepperFest®* symbols take you to join the spicy fun by challenging a chili eater. If the pepper-popping lightweight bursts into flame, you collect a blistering bonus.

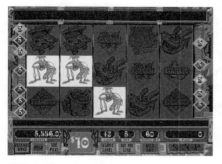

After gathering tasty ingredients, you can hunger for the tasty *TABASCO®* bonus—like Oyster Shooters or Seafood Gumbo—whipped up by zesty Chef Claude. It pays to play the hot games, and this *TABASCO®* game is about as hot as it gets.

68(c). Slapping Mosquitoes scatter screen.

UNCLE SAM® VIDEO SLOTS

Your patriotic spirit will reach new heights in this 5-reel, 15-line game. The Check, State Lottery, and Flag bonuses will offer you true-blue jackpots. With fun animations and upbeat music you will soon be marching in time to play the *Uncle Sam®* video slot machine. This game offers a new twist on tradition. Animated symbols and funky music contribute to a fun—and funny—gaming experience. Did you know Uncle Sam has a *wild* side? The animated symbols and music alone provide an exciting time. The game also provides monumental bonus game action and ways to win. Before we get to these bonuses, check out what the game looks like in Photo 69.

Okay, now you're ready for the fastest check you'll ever get from Uncle Sam, in the Uncle Sam WANTS YOU! bonus round. When three IRS Refund symbols land anywhere on reels one, three, and five, Uncle Sam WANTS YOU to win! There's no wait for this check. The bonus check instantaneously fills the screen and reveals the amount won.

The next great bonus happens in the State Lottery round. We citizens love our scratch-off tickets. Lucky for us, the *Uncle Sam*® game delivers its own version of the ticket-scratching experience. When three State Lottery symbols land consecutively

69. *Uncle Sam*® video slot machine.

on a played line, the State Lottery bonus calls the winning credit number! To reveal the bonus credit win, select three lottery tickets from seven different regions on a map of the United States. If four or five State Lottery symbols land consecutively on a played line, one of the tickets is a bonus credit multiplier. If five State Lottery symbols land consecutively on a played line, not only is there a multiplier ticket waiting to be revealed, there's also a "bonus pick" ticket somewhere on the map. If you find the "bonus pick" ticket, you win an additional 50 credits times the initiating bet. And what's more . . . you also get another pick!

The third great bonus starts in the Flag bonus round. What's better than Old Glory flying high in the air? How about three different flags that represent the chance to win

70(a). IRS Check bonus screen.

up to 100 times the initial wager each spin! When two or more of the same type of flag symbol land consecutively on a played line starting with the far left reel, the Flag bonus begins. The reels on which the initiating flag symbols landed stay in place, while the remaining reels start three free bonus spins. Any new flags that land on the reels increase the bonus win. Check out these bonus screens in Photos 70(a) through 70(c).

The *Uncle Sam®* video slot machine is a game that would make even Betsy Ross proud.

70(b). State Lottery bonus screen.

70(c). Flag bonus screen.

LUCKY LARRY'S LOBSTERMANIA™

I love *Lucky Larry's Lobstermania™*. This is one of my personal favorites. This new 5-reel, 15-line *Lucky Larry's Lobstermania™* video slot machine is clawing its way to your casino floor! The cast of comical crustaceans combines with a barge full of nautical reel symbols for an *iGame-Plus*™ theme that's packed with tasty bonus fun. Break out the drawn butter! The *Lucky Larry's Lobstermania*™ game features a boatload of mouth-watering game play that will make you come back for more. The B-52's song—"Rock Lobster"—plays on the enhanced sound system during each reel spin and the main bonus, adding cool new-wave flair to this appetizing game. This game is very easy to spot because it has a distinctive *Lucky Larry's Lobstermania*™ display mounted on the machine. See Photo 71(a).

Apart from the terrific bonus round that is truly inspired fun in this game, there's also a very money-value worthy scatter pay. The Great Lobster Escape scatter pay is triggered when three, four, or five Caged Lobster symbols land anywhere on the reels. You will chase down the jackpot that results when the lobsters attempt to make their getaway.

The bonus rounds start when Lucky Larry himself makes his in-game debut in the Buoy bonus, which starts when three Lobstermania symbols line up from left to right on any active payline. The game prompts you to select one of the symbols, determining the number of picks you will receive in the main round. Then, it's off to help Larry trawl for lob-

71(a). *Lucky Larry's Lobstermania*™ video slots.

sters. You are asked to pick buoys from the screen and Larry gets down to business, pulling his traps from the ocean floor. Larry removes everything from lobsters to tires to toilet seats from the traps. This old salt Larry offers encouragement to you in his crusty New England accent while the credits pile on to the meter.

In addition to the bonus round and the scatter pays, the

Wild Lobster symbol substitutes for all reel symbols, except the Caged Lobster and Lobstermania symbols, adding more savory payouts to game play. Take a look at these screens in Photos 71(b) and 71(c).

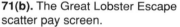

71(b). The Great Lobster Escape scatter pay screen.

71(c). Lucky Larry's Buoy bonus screen.

While this game offers only one bona fide "bonus," which is the Lucky Larry's Buoy bonus, this is offset by the fact that this bonus hits frequently and pays very well. Furthermore, the very good Great Lobster Escape scatter pay combined with the Wild Lobster "wild" symbol on all reels make this one of the very best video slot machines now available. I have played this game many times, very often reached 4,000 and more credits very quickly, and hit the bonus rounds frequently. This is one of the games that I classify in the good money-value category. The only reason why I didn't put this game in my Top 10 is that it has only one bonus.

PHONE TAG™ VIDEO SLOTS

Tag! You're it! You will really "connect" with the *Phone Tag*™ game. This 5-reel, 15-line game is configured to ac-cept wagers up to 20 credits per line for real max bet excitement and player rewards. There's also a 9-line version of this game, with even more great money value. You can see this game in Photo 72.

Bonus Rounds and Top Jackpot

I will now briefly tell you about these bonuses and jackpots, because the game itself has a great instructional screen along with a pay table that tells you more details. I have decided to limit this game's explanation to these few key points primarily because the 9-line game is not available at the time of this writing, but that is the better game for you to look for. Both the 5-line version and the 9-line version contain the same features, and therefore the information I share with you here is also applicable to that 9-line game. Look for the 9-line game to appear exactly as this one, but in a new cabinet. The IGT logo

72. *Phone Tag*™ video slot machine.

will signify that the 9-line game is identical to the 5-line, not something that only looks like it.

- Three Gossip symbols on the first three reels on a played line initiate the Gossip bonus. You are asked to select 1 of 12 characters who calls the next character in the circle, revealing a credit value, a multiplier, or free calls. You can win from 30 to 8,250 credits times the initiating line bet. Now that's something to gossip about!
- The Call Around the World bonus starts when three

or more Call Around the World symbols land in any position on the reels. You get from three to five separate bonus game symbols that spin individually within the larger, stationary reels. Each symbol awards credits, or provides special messages. You can win from 3 to 945 credits times the total initiating bet.

• The top prize is awarded when five Wild Duck phone symbols appear together on a payline with a maximum bet wagered. The quacking phone is a crack up!

And so here we are at the end of "The Best Bonuses" chapter. The games that I have shown here offer some of the best bonuses and bonus structures of all the video slots you will find in the casinos where you play. The bonuses themselves are not the only reason why these games are so good and why they are in this chapter. Many of these games also feature terrific scatter pays and "wild" symbols, and other bonuses-within-a-bonus, and so on, as I described for each individual game. These are features that aren't often combined on other video slots, and therefore it is better for your profitability to look for the games that are detailed here, as well as those in the rest of this book. Each of the games featured in these chapters has something specifically good, with most of them being combined together to provide the best of the money value potential that such video slots are capable of offering. I also wish to point out that almost all these games are offered with the IGT *EZ Pay*™ Ticket System, which is the ticket-in, ticket-out technology for coin-free slot machines. I will discuss this in more detail later, because this is one of the terrific technological innovations that make playing these machines much easier, as well as better, because now you can more easily switch from machine to machine and game to game, without having to lug mountains of coins, or wait for coin fills. This also allows you to better exploit the game's payback, because you will now be able to more easily accommodate one of the key requirements to profitable success, and that is the play of maximum coins. With many machines taking 45 coins, 90 coins, and even 100 coins or more, the fact that these are now "portable credits" makes this one of the key innovations crucial to your skills in successful slot play on these video slot machines. Additionally, many of these games are also available as multi-denominational, which means that you can actually select the value of each credit. This allows you to switch the values of your credits, and that further enhances your skill factors that, together, affect your overall profitability from these wonderful video slots. More on this later, but now let's get back to the games, with the 10 best-paying video slots in the next chapter.

The 10 Best Paying
Video Slots

Each time I create a block of 10 games and give them a new chapter, I make sure to explain that although I classify these machines in these categories, this does not mean that they are somehow "lesser" games because they aren't also listed in the other categories, or in the Top 10. For example, the fact that the games in this chapter are categorized as "best paying" does not mean that the other games in this book are not as good as these as far as pays are concerned. Similarly, just because the games in my previous chapter were categorized as having the "best bonuses" doesn't mean that the games in this chapter or the other games in this book, don't have great bonuses, too. The challenge I have faced throughout this book is precisely how to divide these games into chapters where I can showcase their best features. Well, it wasn't an easy task.

Writing a book about the greatest innovations in casino gaming and games that have occurred since the nineteenth century was not an easy undertaking, particularly when so many really great video slot machines will only be available by the time you are reading this book. The only way that I could accomplish that was to pick about 40 to 50 games that I considered the very top of their class, and the very best of the best, and place those into individual chapters divided by categories that showcase their best attributes. I have done so purely and only to create a format that is easy to read and easy to understand, and tells the story of these video slots in an informative manner and with the single purpose of showing you how you can enhance your gaming experience by selecting the games that best fit what you are after. Together, all this information about all these games forms the foundation of what will become your skills in making powerful profits from playing video slots. Therefore, the *totality* of the information is the *overall* goal of enhancing your profitability and your gaming skills, while each individual chapter is designed to give you more detailed choices from which to build your skills.

I have classified the games in this chapter as best paying because of their high hit frequency, and the many frequent jackpots they offer. They are very fast hitting games. Some have smaller jackpots, others have bigger ones, but together they form the best core of the higher-hit frequency games.

CREATURE FROM THE BLACK LAGOON

Return to those hot summer nights at the drive-in with the *Creature from the Black Lagoon*™ game. Silly scenes of horror from this classic monster movie combine with wisecracking backseat banter of this fun 5-reel, 15-line video slot machine. When I say that this game has "horrible" pays, this means it is **scary** how much it will shower you with credits. I remember my very first horror movie, and that was *The Blob*, starring Steve McQueen in his very first film back in 1958. You see, I'm old enough to remember not only the film, but also the drive-in movie, and Saturday night parking in the back row of the drive-in theater. It didn't much matter what was showing, since most of us weren't watching the movie anyhow, being busy with other more personally exciting pursuits in the backseats of our parked cars. Ahh well, such fond memories of days gone by. Nevertheless, there were times when we did watch the films, and the horror flicks of the day were quite interesting. They were mostly campy and these creature-features weren't really all that scary, but it was fun to watch these monsters hack and claw their way across the screen as hapless humans tried to fight them, all the while the hero chasing the girl for the inevitable happy ending. And so here we are, some 50 years later, and our favorite creature-feature horror films have become a great-paying video slot machine from IGT. Take a look at the "horrible" game in Photo 73.

In addition to the great base pays for this game, there are

73. *Creature from the Black Lagoon™ video slot machine.*

also two bonuses. The Claw bonus starts when three or more Claw symbols line up left to right. You won't need those 3-D glasses as the clawing creature reaches out and shreds the screen to reveal your bonus points. The second bonus is the Snack Lagoon bonus. This starts when four or five scattered snack symbols lead to the concession stand touch-scream bonus. Who knows—there may be a lurking chance to double the tasty total and receive a bonus treat. Enjoy breathtaking animation and enhanced stereo sound as winning line points accumulate. For example, quirky comments accompany classic clips when three or more Creature symbols swim just above the screen's surface. *Oh, no!* The Gill Man has a grip on unsuspecting Kay! Not to worry. This is the third bonus, and it happens when three or more of these symbols line up left to right. The Gill Man then releases poor Kay, then dives back to his lair, revealing screaming bonus points and classic clips from the movie. This game will become a casino floor classic as players "drive in" over and over to see the great monster of myth. Only sneaking your friends into an amazingly "bad" B-horror movie could invoke more campy fun. It's a scream—really.

RISQUÉ BUSINESS™ VIDEO SLOTS

Well, I have to tell you that this game isn't for the faint-hearted. It is definitely an adult game, but it isn't only for the men. There are strippers, of course, but there's something for everyone. This is about the boldest video slot machine there has ever been and it's sure to be the hottest game in town. With four sultry strippers and an array of exciting bonuses, this game will raise some eyebrows and the temperature in the casino. You can give yourself a walk on the wild side with this game. It is a stimulating 9-line, 45-coin video slot machine that features alluring reel symbols and scintillating bonuses. Upbeat dance music plays on the enhanced sound system during game play, adding untamed atmosphere you will love. (See Photo 74.)

The first bonus round starts

74. *Risqué Business*™ video slot machine.

when three or more ATM symbols land anywhere on the reels. You will be prompted to select an ATM machine, which doles out bonus credits—and does so without a transaction fee.

The Strip Tease bonus will surely get a rise out of you when three or more Rod, Lance, Kitty, or Trixie symbols land in any combination on an active payline. You will be asked to pick a dancer from the screen and the steamy fun begins. You will then be prompted to pick three members of the on-screen audience to give the dancer tips. If the crowd is feeling generous, the tips are added to the meter as bonus credits. Is it a tease or will the dancer go all the way? If the group tips the dancer well enough, the dancer removes an article of clothing and the bonus continues. In each round

of the bonus, you are asked to select three new audience members who encourage the dancer to continue. You also receive a lucrative surprise if the dancer takes it all off. With game play like this, it's no wonder that the *Risqué Business*™ game is the most popular club in town.

CLEOPATRA™® VIDEO SLOTS

I mentioned this game in my book *Powerful Profits from Slots*. It is a great game and this new version features 20-line pays. The design and game play are very similar to the one I described in my other Slots book; I refer you to that book for those details. Photo 75 shows you the latest version of the game, which features a 20-line option.

75. The newest multi-line version of the great *Cleopatra*™® video slot machine.

CATCH A WAVE® VIDEO SLOTS

This new *Catch a Wave*® game is one of the great innovations that offer both excitement and great pays. It is a theme reminiscent of all those 1960s "beach" movies, like *Beach Blanket Bingo*, and those with Annette Funicello and Frankie Avalon. It's the kind of cool surfin' safari-style game that will send you back to the days of the sun, surf, sea, and sand. In this game the reels feature animated symbols, a really great wisecracking comical seagull, with lots of other surprises as you play. The reels also include various satirical surfing personalities that animate and speak to amuse you with unexpected and hilarious remarks and quips. This 15-line, 20-coin game can be played for as many as 300 credits per spin, and that adds up to lots of excitement and huge pays! Check this game out in Photo 76.

The first bonus happens when the Big Kahuna free-game bonus is initiated. This turns all the symbols into "scatter" symbols. The bonus credits really rack up as this bonus round continues. The second bonus happens when the Surfboard Club Pick a Board game asks you to select boards from the interactive touch-screen menu. The top jackpot happens when all five of the Catch a Wave symbols land consecutively on an active payline, rewarding you with up to 50,000 credits. The game can be found either as a nickel game or as a multi-denominational game where you can pick the value of your credits. Surf's up, dude! Let's go and party hardy!

76. *Catch a Wave*® video slot machine.

DEEP POCKETS™ VIDEO SLOTS

G'day mate! And welcome to the down-under hip-hop land of *Deep Pockets™* video slots, a 25-line, 125-credit, multi-denomination *iGame-Plus™* machine that features those animated aboriginals—Hapi, Goe, Luki—a land train full of indigenous Oz animal reel symbols, and Roo, a bouncing boomer of a kangaroo, whose bonus game Outback antics will have you feeling like you've gone native. I've spent 15 years in Australia, and I can tell you that it is truly a wondrous land, full of exciting adventure, and even wilder animals. The country is as big as the United States, but with a population of only about 18 million people. Most of these people live in the east, northeast and southeast portions of the country, with some way out west in a place called Perth. The rest of the country is pretty much wild bush. The country spans the temperate zones from the tropical to the sub-

tropical, to the downright cold and snowy mountains of, well, the Snowy Mountains (that's the name, mate). If you get a chance to go there, it's well worth the trip, especially if you also go off the beaten track and get a tour into the heartland, into the real bush country. But, if you can't go, then you can always play this great video slot machine that shows you many of the symbols, features, and animals of Australia. You can take a better look at this game in Photo 77.

77. *Deep Pockets™* video slot machine.

Heads up, mate! Three or more wildly whirling Boomerang symbols on the reels spin up a scatter pay bonus of up to 500 credits. But that's only to whet your appetite for more great credit-generating bonuses. Land three red-and-white-ring target symbols anywhere on reels two, three, and four with less than max lines played and you'll target a bonus win. However, if the three target symbols land with *all the maximum lines* played, Roo the kangaroo creates a three-digit offer by tossing, lawn-dart style, three of his pouches 0 through 9 digits in the *Deep Pockets*™ secondary bonus. By pressing the Keep Win button you get to keep the displayed three-digit offer. But pressing the Modify Win causes Roo to draw an award-transforming "land down under" character from his pocket-o'-plenty—like the digit-rearranging Tasmanian devil, a value multiplying rabbit or a boomerang that returns a new three-digit award. If Roo draws a bomb, the lowest number of the three-digit offer is removed, leaving a two-digit award while another target symbol adds a zero or five to the end of the offer creating a four-digit bonus win.

Nabbing five helmet-goggled Roo symbols on a payline initiates the Outback bonus round. Accompanied by Danny & the Juniors performing that '50s sock-hop fave, "At the Hop," you must lead Roo down successively lower steps to pogo hidden credits, times a last step multiplier, onto the credit meter. You should take a look at these bonus screens in Photos 78(a) and—on the next page—78(b).

78(a). *Deep Pockets*™ Target bonus screen.

With five wild *Deep Pockets*™ symbols on a played line paying a 10,000-credit

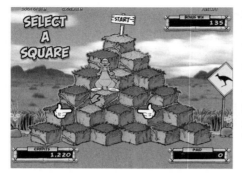

top award and a stoked backyard lawn sport bonus game paying up to 9,875 credits, the *Deep Pockets*™ video slots game will have you yellin' "Crikey!" like a true-blue Aussie!

78(b). Roo Outback bonus screen.

COPS AND DONUTS™ VIDEO SLOTS

The local constabulary in your town may not like this game very much—or perhaps they may like it too much—but it is a great game. It plays on the theme that cops just wanna have donuts, just like girls just wanna have fun. It is a very funny machine. I went to play it in an actual casino just to see how the game plays in real life, as opposed to just at the industry trade shows. I wasn't disappointed. The real-world in-casino game is just as good as its trials. The game I played offered frequent entry into the bonus rounds, with very significant money-value pays along the way as well. I walked away with several hundred dollars' worth of wins after thoroughly enjoying myself playing. Give yourself loads of belly laughs and bonus game excitement with the *Cops and Donuts*™ game. The touchscreen is filled with colorful animated reel symbols that entertain and reward you with frequent hits and the promise of generous top awards. Cleverly animated reel symbols populate the base game, setting the stage for bonus scenarios that arrest the imagination. The *Cops and Donuts*™ game will get the adrenaline pumping faster than flashing red lights in the rearview mirror. Photo 79 captures the criminal fun!

The bonus game situations are a riot, scripted with tongue-in-cheek antics designed to attract an eager "I'm next" audience. It all begins with the Speed Trap bonus. The Speed Trap bonus starts when a cop car appears on the left reel and a speed limit sign stops on the right reel in the same row—and an expanse of highway spreads across the reels in between. Officer Leon arrives on the scene and offers up an unpredictable list of lame excuses for speeding. You get to choose from excuses like, "I gotta get to the liquor store before they close," or "We don't have speed limits on my

79. *Cops and Donuts*™ video slot machine.

planet," and a random selection of equally laughable lines. Each excuse conceals a credit value or a two-times bonus multiplier, and may also contain a free pick in addition to a credit value or multiplier. After three or four excuses are selected from the list, from 4 to 36 credits multiplied by the total initiating bet are awarded.

The Donut Eating bonus is absolutely hilarious. I hit that many times, and each time it's funnier than before. It begins when three Fresh Donuts symbols appear on the first three reels. Officer Chip then introduces the Donut Eating bonus, staged—where else?—in a donut shop! You are asked to take a number to determine how many trays of donuts are awarded, then select trays to reveal credit values. Chip makes humorous comments and noises as he devours the donuts in an amusing display of gluttony. Bonus credits are added to the win meter, and the values of the remaining trays are revealed. You can win from 30 to 690 credits, multiplied by the initiating line bet. The total number

80(a). Speed Trap bonus screen.

of initiating lines then multiplies that total. Photos 80(a) and 80(b) show the bonus screens.

This 5-reel, 20-line *Cops and Donuts*™ game is just the ticket if you're looking for lighthearted entertainment and great game and bonus wins. It can be found with up to 20 credits per line, for a maximum wager of up to 400 credits per spin, with top awards from 10,000 to 200,000 credits. Terrific sound effects, comical dialogue, and familiar music make excellent use of the enhanced stereo sound system. Turn up the volume, and get some coffee with those donuts.

80(b). Donut Eating bonus screen.

THE MUNSTERS™

Add *The Munsters*™ to your list of great video slots, and let television's favorite ghouls add money to your wallet or purse! This fun game evokes memories of our television heritage with animated symbols and original theme music from the show. Exciting computer graphics and enhanced stereo sound combine for a completely ghostly gaming experience. This game is loaded with great entertainment. Herman, Lily, Eddie, Marilyn, and Grandpa symbols frighten the reels at every spin. You will howl with delight when the Wild Bat symbol combines with any character symbol. The Bat turns into a Grandpa character that takes over the entire reel. You won't be able to miss him in his vampirish glory. If you're up to a fright, play this game, shown in Photo 81.

The Munster Match bonus haunts you when five Munster coin symbols land on any payline. You will then be prompted to try and find three matching characters on a grid. Each square yields a value as the characters' identities are revealed.

81. *The Munsters*™ video slot machine.

The credit values for the winning character are totaled for a monstrous payoff. The bonus is doubled if Marilyn is found.

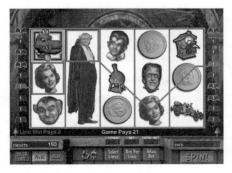

82(a). Wild Bat bonus screen.

If three Spot the Dragon symbols fall on any payline, the game launches the Hot Spot bonus. A real Munsters fan will recognize the hidden staircase that opens to reveal the bonus credits won. The game then plays one of three nostalgic clips of Herman Munster with every big win. What a scream! You can see the bonus screens in Photo 82(a) above and 82(b) and (c) on the next page.

82(b). Munster Match bonus screen.

82(c). Hot Spot bonus screen.

This game can be found as either a 9-line or 25-line version, often with the optional chrome or copper Herman coin topper. This wacky, exciting game will add a new level of fun to your house of horrors, and plenty of profits, too.

83. The newest version of the *Texas Tea*®™ video slot.

TEXAS TEA®™

Texas Tea®™ is a game as big as—well, you know. It's a lot of fun, and I like it very much. In fact, I liked it so much that I described it in my earlier book *Powerful Profits from Slots*. I refer you to that book, in Part II, for the details of this wonderful game. Photo 83 shows you the newest version of the game.

WILD BEAR SALMON RUN™ VIDEO SLOTS

Now here's a totally tasty video slot! The *Wild Bear Salmon Run*™ game is a 5-reel, 15-line video slot machine that can be found with up to 20 credits per line for a total maximum bet of 300 credits. You will land the big jackpot in the Salmon Run bonus, where free spins and an added twist bait big payouts. This game will lure you in . . . hook, line, and sinker. The game tells a true story of some scrumptious salmon and seven hungry bears. There's Fishin' Bear, Ranger Bear, Boone Bear, Jack Bear, Shine Bear, Ace Bear, and Boris Bear. Our story begins with our school o' salmon mozeyin' on over to the place they need to get so they can do what Mother Nature's been tellin' them to do. And our grizzly seven are right there waitin' for 'em.

The game symbols feature nature's food chain at its best. Acorns, pinecones, berries, a pesky raccoon, a trophy deer, and swimmin' salmon, right on up to a ferociously hungry wild bear. Scatter pays award from 2 to 50 times the total bet and there's a top award of 150,000 credits. Take a look at this game in Photo 84.

Hang up the GONE FISHIN' sign and rustle up some credits! When three or more Salmon Run symbols land in any position on the reels, the feeding frenzy begins with the bonus. Ten free spins start automatically, whetting your appetite by tripling all bonus spin line pays. Now each time a salmon lands anywhere on the reels, the catch does not get away. Listen as the game tells a story for one of the seven bears along the top of the screen. Watch as the

84. *Wild Bear Salmon Run*™ video slot machine.

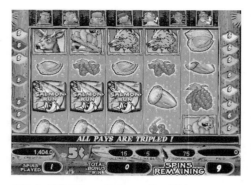

85(a). *Wild Bear Salmon Run™* bonus screen.

credits pile up and salmon swim right on up to one of those hungry bears. The goal is to land seven Salmon Run symbols during the bonus. If you reel in seven of those symbols, all seven bears are fed their first course and you are rewarded with another 10 free spins. The fish and credit feeding frenzy continues until 0 free spins remain or, as legend has it, after a staggering 250 free spins. You can see these bonus screens in Photos 85(a) and 85(b).

So come on, neighbor! Let's go chasing after grizzlies with the great *Wild Bear Salmon Run™* video slot machine game! It's a sure-fire bet we'll catch the one that got away. This game brings the roar of the forest right to the casino floor, and cash-caviar to your wallet or purse.

85(b). Gone Fishin' bonus screen.

SUPER CHERRY®™

Calling all citizens! Fruitville hero *Super Cherry®™* needs volunteers to join a bunch of fruit in their "reel"-life struggle with vegetable mobsters in this 5-reel, 15-line game for the *iGame-Plus™* platform that is a virtual cornucopia of bountiful bonuses. Homegrowns Buff Banana, Perky Pineapple, Sassy Strawberry, Giggling Grapes, and Tempting Tangerine enliven the reels with trellis gossip as Cherry's anti-veggie accessories Skewer, Whipped Cream Gun, and Cutting Board with Knife foil garden plots. Spinning newspapers, whirling helicopter blades, and barking guard dogs announce that Godfather Garlic and his fibrous felons Beanie Brain and Head Lettuce are hosting a jailbreak. In the Call to Arms bonus, you receive bonus credits and cherry power multipliers when superhero Cherry rounds up unruly roughage with free special reel spins.

When posters of Fruitville's most-wanted garden gangstas appear on the reels, the usual suspects are unearthed and put on display in the Line Up bonus. As the villainous veggies shuck and jive, the jailhouse juicer extracts fruity booty from the pulpy perpetrators players pick. Should creaming criminals be this much fun? Does a sundae come with a cherry on top? Fuggetaboudit. Check out this veggie-delight of a game in Photo 86.

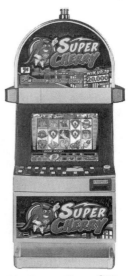

This game is available also on the *Game King*® platform, which is a multi-game video slot machine console, usually with many different games in the menu. It is, however, also offered as a free-standing game, both upright as well as a slant-top. And this, dear friends, brings us to the end of this chapter.

All the games listed here are among those that I have found to pay frequent hits and bonuses, with many being in

86. *Super Cherry*®™ video slot machine.

the very large pays category. As you saw, some of these games can easily pay up to 200,000 credits. Also, most of these games can be found as pennies, so even if the number of lines may be large, the amount of play required isn't as great. And even 200,000 pennies is a good jackpot, plus all the pays in between. But one of the major factors that make these games among the best paying is that many are multi-denominational. This means that you can select the value of your credits. So, if your bankroll can handle it, you can easily play 400 credits as nickels, dimes, even quarters. Then, when you hit that 200,000 credits jackpot, well, it's sure to be worthwhile. Personally, I'm happy even with the pennies because these games hit so frequently that even at that level the real money value can quickly accumulate. And that's why I think these 10 games are among the best-paying video slots.

The Newest Video Slots

In addition to the games that I have shown you so far, there are some others that are so new at the time I am writing this book that they aren't even out of the designers' laboratory. At the Global Gaming Expo in Las Vegas in September 2004, known as G2E, I had the opportunity to see some of these very new games as they were first shown. This particular Expo is only for the gaming industry and is not open to the public, so only those of us who were invited were able to see these games. Some were still undergoing design, and many have not yet been completed. Still, the sample models that I saw there, and played, were so terrific that I think they deserve a mention in this chapter. By the time you read this book most of these games will be on the floor at your favorite casino. But at this time, they are still only in the experimental stages, and many of them awaiting final designs and approvals. Therefore, some of the game details that I mention here may in fact be slightly different, although such changes will most likely be very minor. Okay, this much said, these games will in all likelihood be just like those I am describing here. From my own personal experiences in playing them at the G2E convention in 2004, I am convinced that they will be as successful in the casinos as the other games I have shown so far.

Here then is the newest crop of the greatest video slot machines you are likely to see now, today as you are reading this book, ready for you at your favorite casino. I will describe each game briefly, and show you a photo of the display models of these machines whenever possible. What remaining details there might be about these games will have to wait for another time. One way I can help you is to advise you to look at each game's instructional menu, and look at the Help and Pay Table screens. This will provide you with an overview of the game as prepared by the manufacturer, and although this may not be as detailed as some of the comments and information I am sharing with you in my books, it will provide you at least with some help and a better perspective. Another hint I can offer you is to consider the other information that I have presented in this book, my earlier book on Slots, and my other books as well, because all of that was designed to work together as an overall plan to gain the best profits from all these games, and all casino gaming. I will begin with something that has been part of my life for a long time, a series of films I particularly liked from the 1970s.

STAR WARS®™ VIDEO SLOTS

When the first and original installment in what is now a series of *Star Wars*®™ films first came out, moviegoers everywhere, myself included, marveled at the cinematic skills and special effects that made this fantasy world so real and compelling. With an age-old story of good and evil, a princess, an empire, evildoers, and great heroes, this was a terrific film and a truly mesmerizing experience for the young and old everywhere. Since then, some 30 years have passed, and much has changed in the world, but one thing hasn't changed—our fascination with this film, its premise, and the several films that have now followed in the series. This new video slot machine from IGT makes that world come alive in the casino. You can now do battle with the Jedi Knights, armored troopers, and the Death Star bonus. The base game includes all of the familiar characters and symbols from the Star Wars films. The machine that I played had a giant Death Star mounted at the top, and its tall facade was striking and unmistakable.

In this game there are two basic bonuses. The first is the Death Star bonus, where you get to pilot a ship in an attack on the infamous Death Star. During this bonus you will be prompted to target a ship, or a warrior, and then fire. If you succeed, this bonus will continue for quite a while, reminiscent of some of the old video arcade games. My bonus round lasted almost eight minutes, although some of that time was taken up by the instructions I wanted to read, as well as some time I spent looking at the various options. In all, the average for this extended bonus round is probably two to three minutes. Most likely the final version of this game will have this bonus round shortened a bit, to bring the game more in line with the instant-decision appeal of most slots.

The second bonus is a fight between Obi-Wan Kenobi and Darth Vader. You get a screen where these two characters square off, lightsabers flashing and buzzing, just like in the films. They then proceed to fight each other in a blaze of lights, sound, and glory. If you pick the winner, you win the big bonus credits, and if you don't pick the winner you get consolation credits. Either way you win something, and you get entertained in the process. It's a pretty impressive video slot machine to say the least, and is sure to be a big draw on

87. *Star Wars* video slots.

the casino floor. You can see a picture of this version of the game, at the time I played it, in Photo 87.

LAVERNE & SHIRLEY VIDEO SLOTS

If you were ever a fan of the television show *Happy Days*, you probably also watched *Laverne & Shirley*. Both Cindy Williams, who played Shirley, and Penny Marshall, who played Laverne, went on to great careers in films and television. Penny Marshall actually became a very successful film director, directing the film adaptation of that great television show *The Beverly Hillbillies* (one of my favorite video slots, as I have shown earlier in this book). Both ladies are terrific people on screen and off, and very funny in person. This game is a striking video slot machine progressive, and you can take a look at it in Photo 88.

88. *Laverne & Shirley* video slots, featuring Penny Marshall and Cindy Williams, the actresses who made the TV show famous.

FAMILY FEUD™ VIDEO SLOTS

This is another one of those great television show hits that has found its way onto the casino floor as video slot machines. This is a 5-reel, 15-line machine, with a 75-coin maximum wager, and may be offered as a progressive. The video versions of this game come in two models, one called *Face Off* and the other the *Challenge*. The games feature the authentic-looking game board from the familiar TV show format, which you access through the bonus rounds. For anyone who has seen the television

89. *Family Feud™* video slots.

show, this will be both a familiar as well as entertaining and profitable experience. (See Photo 89.)

ELIZABETH TAYLOR DAZZLING DIAMONDS VIDEO SLOTS

Elizabeth Taylor, the actress and her image, is the classic beauty who inspired this video slot machine. It is a 20-line, 100-coin maximum play video game based around the *Dazzling Diamonds* theme, which is the key to the Dazzling Diamonds bonus. During this bonus you win 10 free spins and a chance at one of two levels of real diamond jewelry. The top jackpot pays 50,000 credits and happens when you line up all five *Elizabeth Taylor* game symbols on an active payline. It's a striking new machine, and you are not likely

to miss it in your favorite casino. You can see the game in Photo 90.

RODNEY DANGERFIELD REEL RESPECT VIDEO SLOTS

What would a casino be without "I get no respect" Rodney? This recently deceased stand-up comedian, television and film star, and international funny-man had performed in casino showrooms for more years than many casinos have been around. Although he liked to quip that he got no respect, the truth was far

90. *Elizabeth Taylor Dazzling Diamonds* video slots.

from it. He got loads of respect from his adoring public as well as the many awards he had won and the laughter he had spread. It was only natural that a video slot machine be created in his image. Regardless of the "I get no respect" quips, you should give this game a lot of respect. This is a 5-reel, 15-line, 75-coin max bet game, full of chuckles and quips from the master of mirth himself. In one case, Rodney is heard saying: "The waitress asked if I wanted some super sex. I took the soup." There are two bonuses, apart

91. *Rodney Dangerfield Reel Respect* video slots.

from the other comical quips. The Paying No Respect reel bonus and the Rodney's Mug bonus are both fun, funny, and no laughing matter. Both bonuses can offer rich rewards indeed. You won't mistake this video slot machine when you see it, as shown in Photo 91, opposite, lower right.

YOUNG FRANKENSTEIN VIDEO SLOTS

If you're too young to remember Marty Feldman, the actor who plays Boris in this remarkably funny and twisted comedy remake of the old classic horror film, then do yourself a big favor and find this film on DVD and rent it, or buy it. Teri Garr who plays the Girl is so funny and cute at the same time. Of course Gene Wilder plays the title role and does it in his now famous underscored style that brings a subtle variety of deadpan humor into the occasional slapstick. His famous denial of who he is—by his over-pronunciation of his name as "Fraaank-en-steen, please!"—will have you in stitches. It's just a great, and very funny, film, and this video slot machine is sure to be equally entertaining. This video slot machine comes in two versions, either as a 5-reel, 9-line, 45-coin max bet game, or the much better 15-line and 75-coin max bet game. The more lines, and the higher the bet you can

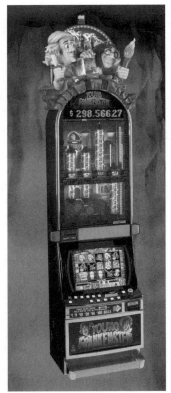

92. *Young Frankenstein* video slots.

make, the better your odds of gaining a decent take-home money-value win. That's why I always like the game versions with more lines and higher credit max plays. Apart from the overall appeal of this game, and the various symbols on the reels themselves and the pays they provide, there is also the Pick a Brain bonus, where you get to pick the Brain for the Monster. The game will play clips from this hilarious movie while you decide which brain to pick. Pick the right brain, and you will be smarter with the great bonus credits win. (See Photo 92 on the previous page.)

THE TWILIGHT ZONE® VIDEO SLOTS

This very eerie television series ran from 1959 to 1964. During its five-year run, this brainchild of television genius and pioneer Rod Serling broke new ground in filmed entertainment, and established the standards for television shows that is still visible today. A huge hit in its day, this show is still being shown worldwide in syndication. Once a year the SCI FI channel shows the *Twilight Zone* marathon over two days, in which all of the episodes are shown from the first to the last. I try to catch the show whenever I can, and even

93. *The Twilight Zone®* video slots.

the episodes I have seen many times entertain again and again. If you have seen the show, then you know what I mean. If you haven't seen it, do yourself a favor and look it up in your TV or cable guide, or go to the video stores and look for the DVD collection. This new video slot machine has all of the television show's familiar themes. It is a 5-reel, 15-line game with a 150-coin max bet option. It has a spinning wheel at the top of the machine, just like some of the other IGT games, like *Wheel of Fortune*®, and *Elvira*® *Mistress of the Dark*™. When you hit the Bonus Zone bonus symbols, this launches you into the wheel bonus. The wheel now spins, and whichever combination it hits will determine the next round of bonuses. You can gain entry into either the Free Spins bonus or the Dimensions bonus. Either way you're a winner, so this game is sure to be popular. (See Photo 93.)

DILBERT'S WHEEL BERT VIDEO SLOTS

The popular cartoon icon of the cube-dwelling office worker gets his revenge in this great new video slot machine. It is a 5-reel, 15-line, 75-coin max bet game that features a spinning wheel at the top, a progressive where available, and two bonuses. The Daily Dilbert bonus shows you three wordless balloons. The words are then filled in and you are asked to pick your favorite cartoon panel, which then reveals the bonus credits. The Wheel of Random Compensation bonus spins the wheel where you can land on a multitude of various bonus credits, each of which is a compensator for your underpaid self. If you know the cartoon, you will know and love this machine, shown in Photo 94.

94. *Dilbert's Wheel Bert* video slots.

THE NEWLYWED GAME VIDEO SLOTS

95. *The Newlywed Game* video slots.

In keeping with a series of video slots based on popular television and game shows, this new video slot machine takes the basis of the trial-by-wedding TV game show that has become so popular worldwide. The bonuses and wins are as big as the hairdos on the television wives of the 1970s, while this 15-line and 75-coin max bet game also takes you into the Wedding Gift bonus. Once in the bonus round you will be offered a series of wedding gifts, wrapped in boxes, and your task is to unwrap them. You do this by touching the screen over the box you want, and the bonus prize in credits will then be revealed. (See Photo 95.)

THE DATING GAME VIDEO SLOTS

Of course, before you get married and join the *Newlywed Game*, you first must find your mate. That's where another staple of the 1970s television game shows comes in, here in the form of a 15-line, 75-coin max bet video slot machine called, appropriately, *The Dating Game.* Again based on the classically camp 1970s innuendos of the television game show, this video slot machine offers you great fun, good pays, and the Blow Me a Kiss bonus. It just could be your dream date, so hurry up and take a look at it in Photo 96.

96. *The Dating Game* video slots, featuring Jim Lange.

THAT GIRL VIDEO SLOTS

Marlo Thomas became a huge star in this 1960s television show, playing Anne Marie, the single career woman living in New York City. At the time, this was a revolutionary concept and a bold step in television programming. The familiar theme song from that show accompanies this new video slot machine based on that TV show. It is a 5-reel, 25-line, 500-coin max bet game, featuring the Fashion bonus and the top jackpot of 50,000 credits when all five *That Girl* symbols are correctly lined up. It's a blast-from-the-past fun game, as shown in Photo 97 on the next page.

97. *That Girl* video slots.

MORE NEW VIDEO SLOTS

Each year the crop of new video slots is getting bigger and bigger. I could go on listing all these new games, but that would not serve the purpose of this book. I wanted to show you not only the new games, but the very best among them, and to do this in a way that would allow you to learn about these games so that you can make better decisions when you play them in the real casinos. To make powerful profits from video slots requires not just the knowledge of the game, but most definitely the knowledge of the choices available. Therefore, I will now provide you with a brief list of some of the other video slots that you will be seeing in the casinos. These are also great new games, and all possess the same characteristics and profiles by which I have identified all the good machines and games throughout this book. I am offering them here for you as a list, without photos, because many of these games are so new that photos of them are not yet available. And so, here are some of the cutting-edge video slot machines that will soon be part of your casino gaming experience.

Hexbreaker Video Slots

This is a 5-reel, 13-payline game with a 260-coin max bet option. It features the Lucky Break and Lucky Ladder bonuses and is based on and around the various superstitions faced by people, such as the Black Cat crossing the road, walking under ladders, and so on.

Ghost Island Video Slots

Another addition to the line of "spooky" games. This one can be found as either a 5-reel, 9-line, or a 5-reel, 20-line game, with up to 20 coins per line max bet. There are two bonuses: the Ghost Island bonus and the Ghostly Ghost bonus. It may be scary, but don't be scared of it.

Wild Taxi™ Video Slots

Take a ride on the wild side. If you've ever taken a cab ride in New York City, then you know the thrills of it. This game is a 5-reel, 15-line, 300-coin max bet video slot machine with a double multiplier symbol and the Go Wild bonus.

Monster Mansion Video Slots

Another in the line of "spooky" slots, this is a "creepy" 5-reel, 25-line, 125-coin max bet game. It features chilling animations and spooky sounds, and the Monster and Lightning bonus.

Benny Big Game Video Slots

A safari-based action game, Benny the Big Game Hunter takes you on a safari through slot action that features the Great Hunter and Elephant Graveyard bonuses. It is a 5-reel game that can be found as either a 9-line or a 15-line game, with up to 20 coins per line max bet options.

Used Cars Video Slots

There's nothing sleazy about this video slot machine, as Salesman Sal is ready to make you a deal! It is a 5-reel game that also comes in either a 9-line or a 15-line format, with up to a 300-coin max bet option. There's the Test Drive bonus and the Sal's Super Sale bonus, during which you will gain credits and are assured of a great deal. There are no lemons in this game, that's for sure. Right, Sal?

Alien Video Slots

Well, if you weren't frightened enough with that now famous series of films, you can get your thrills with this video slot machine based on that theme. No one is going to eat you here. On the contrary, this game is going to give you plenty to smile about. This is a 5-reel, 20-line game with up to a 400-coin max bet option. It offers two bonuses, with the Egg bonus and the Hunt bonus, both based on famous scenes from the films. You may get attacked by Aliens, but this time you will be paid handsomely for the fright.

Joe's Yard Games Video Slots

Backyard barbecues weren't like this when I was young. This video slot machine is a 5-reel, 15-line, 75-coin max bet game with a bunch of zany characters at Joe's backyard barbecue. You can join in with the Balloon Toss and Back Yard bonuses for some succulent credits.

It's a Blast Video Slots

Want some more cartoon fun? Well, how about a herd of wild sheep? This is also a 5-reel, 15-line, 75-coin max bet game, with a Baa Bonus serving up eight free spins using a special set of game symbols, and the TNT bonus in which you are asked to choose from a grid of dynamite sticks that explode and show you your credits winnings.

Shocking Headlines Video Slots

A tabloid explosion in video slots, this 5-reel, 9-line, or 15-line game features a Horoscope bonus in which you get to "Touch Your Lucky Sign," and the Top Story bonus where you get five sub-bonuses. During these you will get to Hide from the Paparazzi, or get the Soap Opera Studs, the Crown Hunt, or the Can You Break the World's Record bonus, or the Reduction or Enlargement bonus. It's a pulp-press bonanza, for sure.

Jackpot Jewels® Video Slots

This is one of the "rich" games from IGT, where you can not only enjoy the 5-reel, 15-line, 300-coin max bet base game, but also gain entry into the lucrative upper-crust bonus round. In the bonus round you will see lots of doors, and you will be asked to pick and choose among them. As long as you pick doors that open and reveal a credits prize, you can keep at it for more and more credits. The bonus will end, however, if you pick the door that shows the "collect" symbol. Even one good pick here is worth some good riches.

Totally Puzzled Video Slots

Like puzzles? Jigsaws? Rubik's cube? Crosswords? This 5-reel, 20-line, 400-coin max bet game is based on games we all remember, including that little plastic "pick and slide" puzzle from family road trips. The *Totally Puzzled* game recreates this in the Pick and Slide bonus, and there's also a free spin bonus. Bring the whole family for this road trip of fun with this video slot machine (but leave the small kids at home, please).

Wild Dolphins Video Slots

Are you ready to flip over this game? Okay, a bad pun—but a good game. This game can be found as either a 9-line, 180-coin max bet game, or the better 25-line, 500-coin max bet game. As you know, the more lines you have and the more credits you can bet in total, the better your wins. That's why I like these kinds of games better than the lesser lines and max credits versions. When you get to the Talent bonus round in this game, the dolphins do tricks that result in bonus credits. Then, in the Pearl bonus, you get to pick a symbol from a variety of choices, and that then animates and reveals your wins. With a top jackpot of up to 400,000 credits, this is sure to be a game many will enjoy for its great pays.

Kingpin Bowling Video Slots

Looking for a perfect 300? Well, now you don't have to roll the pins at the local bowling alley to get it. All you need is this new 5-reel, 25-line, 500-coin max bet video slot machine, and the perfect 300s will add up to cash winnings. This game offers loads of bowling-themed features, including two very funny bonuses. In the Bowl bonus, you will roll for credits, including strikes, spares, and gutter balls, over a span of 10 frames in this bonus round. In the Gobble Wobble bonus, when the wobbling pin knocks over other pins you will get even more credits. Break out the corduroy and spandex, curl the hair, and let's head for the bowl.

Five Times Pay™ Video Slots

This is a video version of the very popular reel slot machine game. This version is a 3-reel, 9-line, 45-coin max bet game where the Five Times pay symbols add more credits to your wins, much like the reel slot machine with which you may already be familiar. If you haven't seen one of these Five Times reel slots before, please look it up in my earlier book, *Powerful Profits from Slots*.

Mystical Mermaid Video Slots

Various denizens of the sea will swim into your life by bringing bountiful gifts of fortune as you play this new

5-reel, 20-line, 400-coin max bet game. In the Big Splash bonus, you can win up to 40 free spins with double payouts. The Top Jackpot also pays not just the 10,000 credits for the line win, but also 4,000 credits for the scatter pay, and also awards you an extra 40 free spins at the double pay rate. Old Neptune, King of the Sea, would be proud.

Nurse Follies Video Slots

Well, we've all heard of the Folies Bergere, of the Ziegfeld Follies of old Broadway, and now here come the *Nurse Follies*. This new 20-line, 400-coin max bet game is sure to keep you in stitches as the nurses run amok on your spinning reels during the Daily Funnies bonus. And if you've ever been overcharged for your hospital stay, you will know what is coming in the Hospital Charges bonus round—except that here you are the beneficiary of the billing mishaps and earn bonus credits. A cut above the rest, this hospital humor video slot machine is an easy pill to pop, and loads of cash to win.

Triple Double Dollars™ Video Slots

This is another video derivative of the very popular reel slot machine, featuring these bonus symbols. This video version has three reels, with nine lines, and a 45-coin max option. If you would like to know more about the reel slot machine version upon which this game is based, please refer to my earlier Slots book.

Triple Stars® Video Slots

This video version of the popular reel slot machine takes the spinning reel slot theme to stellar new heights. It is a 3-reel, 9-line, 45-coin max bet game, with the Falling Star bonus round that adds variety to the traditional reel-spinner look of this video game.

Spin 'n' Hold Video Slots

Finally, there is a new series of video slots that look, play, and feel completely different from anything you may have experienced before. These are called the *Spin 'n' Hold* video slots, and they combine the principles of video poker with the reel spinning slots. Using many of the established game names and game symbols, such as *Double Diamond®* and *Wild Cherry®*, this series of new games also offers a derivative of the popular video slots themes of *Cats 'n' Dogs®* and *Little Green Men®*. The way these games are configured is truly inspired. I played several of these at the Gaming Expo, and I can tell you they are not only loads of fun, but provide you with some of the best options for skill-based games on reel slots. Here's how it works.

Just as in video poker, your first spin lands a combination of symbols. While video poker deals you five initial cards, here the machine will land three symbols on the three reels, one symbol on each reel, just like the traditional reel slot machines. But this is a video slot machine, and this is not the end of the game; it is actually the beginning. You see, these *Spin 'n' Hold* games have a video tiered tower, just like many of the multi-hand video poker machines. Once you receive the initial spin, you can then hold any one, two, or all three of the game symbols, and spin the reels on the additional tiered tower of reels. Depending on the game, there are usually at least four extra game screens where the symbols you held on the initial spin are repeated, and then the non-held reels spin again, providing you with many more chances to make a winner, or a better winner. Just as in video poker, if you are initially dealt a winner, you can hold that winner and all of the hands on the multi-game video poker machine now also hold those winners. Similarly, if such a video poker machine were to deal you only a small winner, you can hold that and the held cards are repeated on all the hands yet to be completed on the draw. This way you can make a better winner from a small winner, or make a non-winning deal into a winning one.

This is the same principle behind these new video slots, except that here you are holding symbols instead of cards. So, just like in video poker, if this video reel machine deals you a winning spin, you simply "hold" all the winning symbols and they are repeated on all played lines, and so you win that many times the pay. Also just like these multi-hand video poker machines, on these new *Spin 'n' Hold* video slots if you are dealt a small winner on the initial deal, or a non-winner on this initial spin, you can then choose to hold some of the symbols, and go for a better win on some of the other lines. Basically, you get to give yourself many more chances to gain a better winner, or to make an initial non-winning spin into a winner. This takes the world of the reel slot machine directly away from the realm of a purely passive

98. *Double Diamond*® *Spin 'n' Hold* video slots.

game, where the only skills you can exploit are your game selection skills, bankroll management, and slot strategy play skills. These *Spin 'n' Hold* games allow you to practice very similar skills to those you normally use for video poker. You get to choose which symbols to hold and which not to hold, and respin the game for other, or additional, hits. As in video poker, the skills you have in the ways you pick your holds and discards will gain you the better winners.

As a basic strategy tip, always hold all dealt winners, always hold both like-kind symbols, and always hold the *highest*-paying symbol when no others are available. When you have the option to hold either a wild, or a doubler, symbol, always hold *only* that one if you don't have any of the top three award symbols along with it. This is about as simple as I can make it at this time. Take a look at the four games that I played at the Gaming Expo, here in Photos 98 (opposite), 99 and 100 (on this page), and Photo 101 on the next page.

And that, dear friends, are all of the newest and best video slots now available, and those that are making their way to your favorite

99. *Wild Cherry*® *Spin 'n' Hold* video slots.

100. *Cats 'n' Dogs*® *Spin 'n' Hold* video slots.

101. *Little Green Men® Spin 'n' Hold* video slots.

casino as you are reading this book. Now that I have listed them all, I will explore some other aspects of play that combine to make the powerful profits premise a reality in the majority of playing situations.

Keys To Winning

In most of my books in the *Powerful Profits* series I write a chapter on the Keys to Winning. There are many different means and methods to employ, each applicable to different aspects of each game. Every time you wish to play any casino game well, and lose less while making more, it is rather like starting a new job. While it is not my intention here to teach you gambling so that you can play casino games and gamble for a living, as if it were your job, the analogy as it applies to the knowledge required can work quite well. My intent here is simply to show you that you can relax, have fun, enjoy your gaming vacation, and still do much better on the casino games, and on video slots, than you would have otherwise, and certainly better than many tens of thousands of others who will play video slots, or the other casino games, without this knowledge, information, and skills. Naturally, if you do want to make casino gambling your job, and wish to learn all the details, then I refer you to my book *Powerful Profits: Winning Strategies for Casino Games*, wherein you will learn how to do this.

141

For now, just use the analogy as your guide into the world of successful casino play, one with fewer losses and greater profits than before.

Video slots are great games and are among the very few casino games that can actually be played for significant money-value profits. Playing these games can be a rewarding as well as exciting experience. While I can show you what to do, and how to do it, and explain why it is better to do it this way, the actual doing of it, and your *success* in the doing of it, will depend on you. Some people can have great intellect, and can learn many things, and can even teach them, but aren't very good at doing them. Others are very good at the doing, but would be hard-pressed to explain just exactly *how* they are doing it, and *why* they are successful at it. All this simply means that we are all different, and no two of us will have the same success, or do the same thing the same way, even if we all learned the same things together. That's why I always include this chapter on Keys to Winning. This is the blueprint for the greatest possible success. These "keys" are the glue that holds all the rest of the information together. Whereas the remainder of this book is all about video slots, and the various means of playing, recognizing the better games and, later, strategies, without these Keys to Winning, all this would be so much loose information without much cohesiveness. You see, the main reason why these keys are so important is because they deal with the "human factor." Us. We. The people. These Keys to Winning not only concentrate on the game itself, but especially on our relationship to that game, or games. It is this personalized approach that allows us to gain the maximum benefit out of all of the other information we learn. We are co-joined by these keys in a mutual tapestry of knowledge, and the derived ability to apply that knowledge to our gaming success. We may not all do equally well, but we will all have the necessary background to do well, and to improve as we experience. I have, therefore, made these Keys to Winning as closely applicable as possible to the widest range of common experiences. Consequently, everyone should be able to gain the mastery of the casino gaming experience, and understand what this is, and how these keys apply.

In my books *Powerful Profits from Slots* and *Powerful Profits from Video Poker*, I have written extensive chapters on the Keys to Winning, as these apply to slot machines. Since video slots are also slot machines, many of those keys also apply here. To accommodate as many readers as possible, I will present, in this chapter, a shortened digest of the Keys to Winning from the basics shown in complete details in my books on Slots and Video Poker. I will select, and modify, only those categories that apply specifically to video slots.

KEYS TO WINNING FOR VIDEO SLOTS

Yes, it is true that slot machines are machines, that they are preprogrammed to pay on certain pays, appear to run in certain cycles, are set to pay back certain percentages, and so on. Yet, if no slot machine ever paid a jackpot, no one would play them, and casinos as we know them wouldn't exist. Therefore, to be a winner, and to win more often than most people, you must apply your powers of *choice* and combine this with the other categories I list below. By reading this book and learning what is shown here, you are on your way toward becoming an *informed* player, and therefore a *better* player, whose luck is *calculated* and not merely a blind act of good fortune. There is a lot more to being a winner playing video slots than many people imagine.

To most people the slot machine is merely a simple device into which you stick some coins, or currency, push the play button, and then see if you won something. Although this is the most basic principle of how the video slot machines function, this is not the only item of knowledge you should possess when playing them. Blind luck happens, and it happens frequently. I have seen people come to Las Vegas who have never been to a casino or even seen a video slot machine. They are flabbergasted. They are overwhelmed. Everything is new to them. Innocently they walk up to some machine that could be among the worst games available, with the highest house edge, insert a dollar, or five dollars, or some coins in those few machines that still take them, and presto! Here comes the jackpot! Unbelievable, right? Yes, and no. Sometimes even these people don't realize that they have won something. As odd as this may sound, I have seen casino executives desperately trying to convince such novice video slot players not only that they did not break the machine, but that they actually won a big jackpot. Many such people are just so "green" that they need such convincing. Of course, after they are convinced, then the reality sets in, and all of a sudden they are video slot players. From that point on they think that winning at video slots is easy, and they try again. And again. And again. And, often, no such luck ever again happens for them. And therein lies the greatest problem with video slot players: They don't learn from their past experiences, or the experiences of others they have known, or heard about. All they can see, or remember, is that one time they were really *this* lucky, but not all the other times when they were *not* lucky. Most of all, they never realize that luck like this is like a blind squirrel finding an acorn once in a while. Once in a while such blind luck happens, but there are long "whiles" in between such happenings, and they may never happen to you again. Such people not only did not learn from their experiences, they did not even know that any learning is necessary. And they did not pursue any such knowledge even after repeatedly trying to recapture that "luck" and failing to do so. Even the most rudimentary information, such as that offered by most major casino resorts in the hotel rooms, is better than nothing at all. Although most of this information isn't exactly helpful, because it mostly talks about how to play the games which that casino happens to offer, and not necessarily about how to play these games *well*, nevertheless even this information is more knowledge than such novices have. Unfortunately, many such people will ignore even that little knowledge.

Although this example of the really green novice—and such blind luck—may be extreme to some extent, it serves to illustrate a wider problem among video slot players—and particularly for video slot players because of the increasing variety of such video slots and the tremendous playing options they offer, each of which requires a dedicated and knowledgeable decision on the part of the player. Even players who have been to casinos several times, and are now familiar with video slots—how they work, and how to play them—and may even possess some of that rudimentary knowledge from the in-room pamphlets, or booklets, or merely from information obtained through conversations with other players, even these people do not necessarily behave, or play, in any more profitable manner than did those very "lucky" novices. Just because you have been to a casino and have played slots before, or perhaps even video slots, doesn't mean you already know all you should know. Maybe you have won. Maybe you have lost. Perhaps you have won and lost, and are about even. What if you only lost a little? Does that make you feel comfortable about your casino slots expertise?

Being "comfortable" is an important concept. Many people feel "uncomfortable" in the beginning, either because they are green novices, or because they have only recently become familiar with casinos, the casino environment, and video slot machines. As with most things we do, there is what is called a "learning curve." This simply means the time it takes most of us to learn at least the very basics of whatever it is we are planning to do, or are doing. Once that is achieved, then there is another concept commonly known as the "comfort factor." This is the point we reach, eventually, after having done whatever we have contemplated through the learning curve process. We reach this point of the comfort factor when we have had direct experiences with that particular situation and found either that we liked it, that it was good, that it was profitable, or that it didn't really hurt that much. When we "like" something, it's usually because it does something for us that is pleasing, such as being entertained by the experience with the video slot machine. Whenever we think that something was "good," this usually means that the entertaining experience we liked so much also proved rewarding in some way. This leads us to the part we call "profitable," and although this normally means that we made some money, with video slot machines this could be as simple as having received a pay. Any pay. Even a small pay that, in reality, meant an overall loss. But just the act of getting it, with the other factors combined, often results in our *perception* that this was profitable, in which case we usually think of "profit" as something in addition to mere money. The casino experience, for example. Or the camaraderie among players. Or the fact that we were there with a loved one and shared a happy time, overall, which had little to do with the act of profiting from this particular video slot machine. Maybe we reached the comfort factor after having lost money, but we got some play for it, and therefore the other factors in this human equation were satisfied, and, consequently, we thought about this as the "payment" for that series of experiences. Even though we lost money, we still feel okay about it because it "didn't hurt that much." For most people, the loss of money is a "hurtful" experience, but many people become resistant to that feeling after having played video slots for a while, or several times. They quickly come to find out that the loss of money is an integral part of the playing experience. No one will win all the time. Losing is just as much a part of the playing of video slot machines as is winning. And losing happens a lot more often.

Once we all start to realize these human factors, we have come to the comfort zone, that point in our psychological approach to slot playing where we are no longer in wonderment about the game and no longer in fear about the loss of our money. As a video slot player, when you reach this point of familiarity with the game, and the comfort level regarding the experience, the money, the game, the winning, and the casino environment, then you have developed what can be described as "casino familiarity," or perhaps "gaming resilience." Either way it means largely the same thing: You are no longer a novice, and the act of playing video slot machines no longer scares you. Now you have a decision to make, and a very important one. You can continue being happy with what you know, continue to play the machines with this minimal familiarity, and "hope for the best." This will place you in the same class as the vast majority of casino video slot players who have reached this point of familiarity with the game and continue to try for the stroke of blind luck. These are the video slot players who feed billions of dollars into the casino's coffers, and these are the people who are very largely responsible—to the tune of around 80 percent of all the casino revenue—for the cumulative huge losses suffered by casino video slot players every year. If you really think about it, the numbers are staggering. In Nevada alone, casinos "win" over $9 billion each year. Yes, that's *billion*, with a "b." Nine times one thousand millions. Of dollars! And growing each year. Of this, some 70 percent comes from video slot players. This is a total cumulative loss of around $6.3 billion. In Las Vegas, the total casino "win" for a recent year was around $5.2 billion. That's combined among all the casinos in the Las Vegas area, about 100 or so casino resorts and casino hotels. Over the approximately 32 million visitors, the average bankroll was around $670. Among those who call themselves gamblers, the average bankroll was closer to $1,200 for the "bring with you" money. On exit, it turns out that most of the players actually accessed additional funds, which brought the average per-player "loss" to about $3,200.

The point of all this is to show you how easily the "comfort factor" translates into huge financial losses. As a consequence, if you continue to be happy about all that you already know, or think you know, about the playing of video slot machines, then you will be part of this great mass who lose that average amount each time they come. And notice also that this is an average *loss*, and not an average win. There's a big difference between them, in reality and in concept. The truth is that a smaller portion of these slot players will lose many millions, while the majority will lose a lot more than the few hundred, and a smaller portion will lose about the average, or less. But the fact remains that *they all lost!*

Therefore, the second decision you must make for yourself is whether you want to "graduate" from merely the comfort level and reach a point of "expertise." To become an "expert" at playing video slots doesn't mean you have to become a professional gambler, or even an author of gaming books. It simply means that you take the time to learn more than the "average Joe," and give yourself the ability, and the knowledge, to not merely lose the average player loss, but to actually join the very elite club of players who win. It *is* possible to win, you know. And no, you don't have to trust to blind luck, and you don't have to stumble around in the dark looking for that acorn. People like me, who write books on gambling, are sort of like your seeing-eye dog. We lead the way. We point to the right things, and show how to do it the better way. This doesn't mean it is the only way, or even the right way. This simply means that from all our years of dedicated research, of playing, of living this life, we have acquired more than the average Joe's amount of knowledge, and are now able to apply it to suggestions and recommendations that we consider valuable. I am writing this book, and my other books in this series, for the purpose of imparting upon you the knowledge it took me more than two decades to accumulate. I am well aware that the "learning curve" can be difficult to overcome, while the "comfort factor" is easily reached. Therefore, I seek to simplify the information, make it as clear as I can, with as much impact as is possible to impart to it. By investing your time in reading this book, you have shown that you have the desire to improve yourself as a video slot player and reach a level of expertise. This is the second of the two choices I described, and you have made it right here. It's not easy. Simplicity belies complexity. Video slots aren't just mere diversions. They are serious gambling games that can, and will, take your money if you don't know what to do, and how to do it to the best level the game allows. To learn this takes time, and the willingness not just to learn it, but also to apply it, and apply it correctly. To help you do this, I have therefore created the Keys to Winning. These are, in order of importance as I see it, as follows:

Knowledge
Patience
Bankroll
Selection
Discipline
Win Goal

For those of you who have already read one or more of my books, this list may seem familiar. These Keys to Winning are universal and apply equally well to all casino games. However, in each of my books I direct these points specifically as they apply to the game, or games, that are the subject of that book. So, while these keys are the same for slots, blackjack, craps, video poker, and the other games about which I have written, the *details* apply specifically to video slots. My point here, in this chapter, is to let you in on the "secret" that will allow you to become *more secure in your gaming*, more steady in your approach, more confident in your end result, and more conscious of your expectations. And these are the real secrets to your success in playing video slots.

KNOWLEDGE

This should be relatively easy. This is the "learning curve," the decision to improve yourself, and probably the reason you bought this book. Knowledge means to learn as much as possible, with as clear a direction toward your end goal as possible. Knowledge means to know not just that video slot machines exist, or what they look like and how to play them, but also how to play them *well*. Playing these many different varieties of video slots well also means incorporating into your knowledge all the other principles of these Keys to Winning. Knowledge is growth in understanding and in continual improvement. All of this is necessary to achieve more than just blind luck in your gaming. Learning it will have a direct and positive impact on your play, and on your life, and specifically on how you approach the video slot machines the very next time you visit a casino.

PATIENCE

I am often surprised at how easily people get upset over the casino games they choose to play, and slots and video slots in particular. They get upset when they don't hit. They get upset when they do hit but don't think it's enough. They get upset if they don't hit the jackpot. When they hit a secondary jackpot, they get upset that they didn't hit the top jackpot. And when they hit the top jackpot, unless it's something in the millions, they get upset as to why they couldn't hit it sooner. Are you this kind of player? Does this fit your slot-playing profile? If it does, then you aren't patient. You are hyper. You shouldn't play slots, and particularly video slots at all. Playing video slots can be a very prolonged experience, one which will require your utmost patience. Wins will happen, and although sometime you may be lucky and get that good win right away, most of the time it will not come that easily. You will have to work for it for a while. This may require you to do several sessions, and perhaps even visit several casinos. It could mean that you will have to make several trips before you achieve that desired win goal. Setting achievable win goals is part of the art of patience. I call it the "art" of patience because that's what it is. Patience is not a skill, and it is not science. It is art. Skills can be learned. Science can be learned. But you must be born with the ability to be patient. You cannot learn to be that way. Fortunately, almost all human beings are born with that ability. The vast majority of us are born with the ability to learn languages, to deal with our environment through our senses, and to find out how to survive. These are all inherent abilities. We also have the ability to be patient. Unfortunately, the pace of our modern world rarely rewards patience, at least visibly. Although most achievements we see publicly are the result of hard work and a lot of patience, by the time we see these achievements they have already happened. To us, these seem as if they happened overnight. The old story among actors who finally gain star status goes something like this: "After 30 years of acting, suddenly I'm an overnight success." This is also true for many other disciplines, including the writing of books.

These examples demonstrate that success playing video slots is not merely that once-in-a-lifetime blind-luck event. You can be successful as a player each time you play, overall throughout your career as a player, but only if you develop your art of patience. Notice I said *develop*, rather than acquire. Like the ability to draw, you must practice and learn, and learn from doing, and learn from mistakes. It won't be easy, but then nothing worthwhile ever is. Developing patience means that you will curb your natural reactions. These are the emotional bursts, such as exuberance when you win and anger when you lose. Both are the extremes along the scale upon which the pendulum of your slots success swings. First, the trick to developing the art of patience when playing video slots is to realize that great and glorious wins *will* happen. Also, to realize that equally great and horrendous *losses* will happen. Both are the extremes along the pendulum of life's probabilities. Second, develop your ability to curb your reactions to those extremes. Be happy when you win, but remember that this is not an event that will always happen like this. Don't start expecting this every time. Remember that the money you *don't* lose back today will spend very nicely tomorrow, with a cooler head and a clearer perspective. When you lose, at the other extreme end of the spectrum, curb your reaction equally. Don't start to question yourself beyond reason. If you feel you have forgotten some part of your knowledge, by all means look it up. See if you were correct, and if so, learn from the experience. When you realize that you did everything correctly, and still suffered that great and horrendous loss, then curb your instinct to blame everything and everyone, and try not to destroy yourself or the solid foundations of your playing abilities. Remember that this is just the other extreme of the spectrum, and that in this instance, the pendulum of overall probability simply swung against you. It will swing back. That's the reality, and it will always happen like that.

It may take what you consider a long time. The phrase "a long time" means to us, as human beings, something entirely different than to the universal event statistics. What you may consider as "a long time," may in reality only be a tiny fraction of a micro-second in the overall scope of universal time. It depends. It's all relative. If you play for two hours and you don't reach your win goal, was that losing streak "a long time"? Well, for you, perhaps. But you should be conscious of the fact that the universe doesn't revolve around your particular perception of reality, or length of time. Patience, therefore, is the art of being able to react to each situation *without overreacting to it*—and that's where the greatest benefit lies. You will have to work this out yourself, because no two people deal with the same set of circumstances in exactly the same way. It is important that you understand these factors, because patience will not only enable you to play the video slots better, but will allow you to reach your comfort level far quicker and with far more positive results. By realizing that patience is a requirement for enjoyment, and profit, from your video slot play, you will become far more at ease with the process. This will relax you under a variety of circumstances and situations, and will in turn allow you to take a far more rational, and less emotional, approach to playing video slots.

BANKROLL

All of these Keys to Winning are important, but bankroll is perhaps the foremost. The reason is quite simple. Without money, you can't gamble. Gambling is all about money. Losing money and, of course, winning money. You must have it to start. You can't start without it. Even credit is money, and so is a credit line at the casino. It doesn't matter how you acquire your money, but whatever money you bring with you, or send to the casino cage, or get in credit at the casino, whatever money that is, constitutes your bankroll. This is the money you have designated as your gambling money. Your gambling stake. It should not be money you need for your family's rent, mortgage, food, clothing, health care, and so on. This should be accumulated "spare" money, something you can afford to lose without such a loss having a devastating impact on you and your family. Any gambling bankroll should be made up of money that you have designated as *expendable*. This doesn't mean that it should be treated as already lost, and hence treated recklessly. After all, it's still your money. It is still important money and should be highly regarded. It was your work that made it possible. Just because you designated it as your gambling money doesn't mean it has suddenly lost its value. It still spends just the same. Many people make the classic mistake of setting aside their gambling money with the conviction that it's already gone, dead, done, lost, and therefore it means nothing. Wrong! This is a defeatist attitude. Thinking like this will result in two inevitable occurrences. First, you have already convinced yourself that you are a loser, that you will lose, and therefore this money is already lost. You will therefore gamble recklessly, without thought or regard to the value of the money or the consequences of your reckless actions. As a result, you will lose and this will reinforce your conviction that "Ah, well, it was already lost. I knew it." So, you will be happy in your loss, because you convinced yourself that it was inevitable. Second, you will not play knowledgeably, and certainly not in concert with these Keys to Winning. Thus, again, you will lose. When you do, this becomes yet another reinforcement of your initial starting attitude. "So," you now say to yourself, and quite possibly to anyone who will listen, "it was only gambling money. I knew I was gonna lose it, so what? It was my 'mad' money, anyway. Ah, well. Maybe next time." You have now thoroughly convinced yourself that you are a loser and justified your initial defeatist attitude by making sure that you lost. If this is how you think, you should never even go to a casino. This kind of an attitude has no place in life, and certainly no place in gambling.

Your bankroll is your lifeline. It is essential. It should be treated valuably, protected, and handled with care. In addition, it must be sufficient to carry the weight of your action. Many people go to play video slots and bring a bankroll that is far less than what is required to start any kind of play on even the lowest-of-the-low machines and games. Not only that, these people take that meager bankroll and go for the big, expensive video slots. They start with the 500-coin per pull and higher denomination machines, or even higher than that. That's like jumping off a building without a parachute and hoping that the landing on the hard ground won't hurt all that much. Don't be like that. If you go to the casino to play video slots, or whatever you are going to play, take enough money with you so that your starting bankroll is at least sufficient to support your expected action, as that applies to the specific game or games you will choose, and at the levels that you can afford to play. Don't play video slots whose action requires $500 dollars as a session bankroll if all you have is a $100 stake. If you do, you will lose it quickly, or will be forced to play at less than maximum coins and that in itself will be a prescription for disaster, most of the time guaranteeing that you will lose. The amount of your bankroll should be determined by several factors. First, it depends on what this money means to you at that time. If this money is truly unencumbered, then you will feel a lot better about making it a true bankroll. If this money is not completely unencumbered, such as when a portion of it could be used for something else, but that something else is not one of the essentials to survival, then maybe you will not handle the bankroll as well, or it may not be big enough. As a general rule, any gambling bankroll should always be made up only of entirely unencumbered money, and no part of it is needed, or could be even considered as being needed, for something else. Unencumbered money is free and not scared. Encumbered money will always be scared money, and in gambling, scared money will fly away quickly. Playing with scared money means you are afraid to lose it. This doesn't mean that you have adopted the defeatist attitude we have discussed earlier. This simply means that you have allocated at least some part of your bankroll either as an inadequate amount, or being encumbered upon something else—borrowed from a credit card, maybe, which means you will have to pay it back, perhaps at great stress to you, or your family. This is a very bad way to start your bankroll. Always start your bankroll with free money, which will become a solid gambling stake and not frightened at the prospect of being lost.

Second, the amount of your bankroll should be determined by the kinds of machines you intend to play. If you want to play nickel video slots that take 45 coins as max play, remember that this equals $2.25 per pull. Your bankroll should therefore reflect that action. If you want to play higher limits than that, your bankroll should certainly be equally higher. If you plan to play "penny" video slots, but these require 400 coins as max bet, remember that this is $4, not just pennies! Your bankroll must, therefore, reflect the fact that you are playing a $4 machine! And if you play a nickel game that takes 500 coins per pull, remember that this is $25 per pull and that, therefore, you are a very high roller when it comes to slots, and especially the video slots. Your bankroll must be big enough to adjust to that. In addition, whatever your intended action, your bankroll should be adequate to withstand fluctuations, not only in your fortunes as you play, but also in your decisions concerning the *kinds* of games you will play. Your bankroll should have a "slush" factor, allowing it to withstand the necessity for such on-the-spot decisions. What if you saw another kind of machine, perhaps one you have read about here, and decided to play that instead? Your bankroll should be adaptable to such deviations from your initial starting strategy.

How do you arrive at the bankroll figure? Hard to say. It's all individual to each player, and to you. You know yourself, and your circumstances. All I can do is offer you *guidelines*, with the hope that you can intelligently adapt this guideline to your specific situation. Most of the time, if you plan to play about three hours per day, for an average of three days, then I can suggest that for the majority of nickel-based video slots that take up to 45 coins per pull you will have to gather a bankroll of at least $200 per session. For those that take 90 coins per pull, take $400 as your session bankroll. For games that take $4 and more per pull, regardless of whether they are "nickels," "pennies," or whatever, take a minimum of $500 per session. Without these kinds of stakes you will never be able to play the games to their optimum payback or gain the maximum benefit from the pays and bonuses they offer. Playing for less than these suggestions, and for less than maximum coins, will simply mean that you will lose your money. It may take you longer to lose it, but lose it you will, and that's a fact. You can't win if you don't play properly, and the only way to play these video slots properly and profitably is to always have at least the minimum session bankroll amount, to always play the games with the max bet wager, and to always keep in mind the money-value hits that translate into your take-home-and-leave profits.

SELECTION

This is the part where "skill" in video slot play comes into the picture. Many people believe that when playing video slots winning is purely dependent on luck. Although it is correct that most video slots are a passive game and, therefore, you cannot control the outcome of the event—except for some of the newest games I mentioned in the previous chapter—it is not correct to say that playing video slots involves no skills. I don't mean merely the skills of being able to operate the machine that contains the game. I am referring to skills such as game selection, machine selection, brand name selection, game detail selection, size of the wager selection, payout hierarchy selection, credit versus coin play selection, play methodology selection, size of bankroll selection, play duration selection, time when to play selection, casino where to play and what kinds of machines to play there selection, and the remaining variety of various applied skills you will acquire as you continue reading this book, and then put your own abilities into practice. There is a lot more to being a winning video slot player than just showing up in the casino, sticking your money in the machine, and pushing the play button. Each of these selection skills is part of the "learning curve," and "comfort zone," which all of us have to reach. By acquiring these skills, you can become not only more knowledgeable, but also more comfortable. You will find that you are no longer a victim to the mere chance of luckily selecting just the right machine, at the right time, and for the right reasons. You will now actually be able to approach your casino visit with the ability to look for the kinds of games that you know are among the better options, and do so with a solid plan of attack. Not only will this result in more confidence and comfort when you play, but it will directly translate to regular profits. Although you won't win every time, or perhaps achieve your win goal every time you play, you will now be able to realize that this is a part of the overall approach to the game. You will no longer be a victim to emotional swings, such as deep disappointment when you don't win, or reckless exuberance when you do. Although curbing these emotional reactions is part of patience, as discussed above, and also discipline, discussed below, the selection skills will contribute to your overall Keys to Winning in a way in which the video slot machines will no longer hold the "secret," but will divulge it to you, because you now know what to look for and how to do it to your best advantage.

Now let's take a look at some of the selection skills in more detail. Remember that each is part of an overall whole, and even though each is important, the sum of the whole is far more crucial to your winning success at playing video slots than any single part. Often you will have to make adjustments, even while you are playing, because in the real world not all of these skills will apply all the time. Neither will all of the advice I am offering here, nor the guidelines. However, all this information, *viewed together*, forms the sum total of what will eventually become your video slot–playing expertise.

Game Selection

A very important skill, which can be acquired through the knowledge part of these Keys to Winning. Notice that while patience was an "art," these are "skills." Anyone can learn these skills. All it takes is the desire to be a winner, the ability to understand the information being offered, and the ability to apply that knowledge to gaming success. Game selection includes several items. What kind of machine? What kind of game? Which denomination? And so on. As with all these skills, the answers to these questions are all part of the *overall* picture. Your success in playing video slots depends on *all* of these abilities. What kind of machine, game, and denomination may be determined by your bankroll, interest, and win goal. Other factors will influence how you approach the other skills among the skill of game selection. Generally, you should select a machine that is without penalty or disadvantage to your win expectation and potential jackpot and bonus awards. This is the simplest and best advice to get you started. From this point on, your skills will dictate further advancements in your play. The machines and games I listed in the previous chapters are the best guideline for all of these considerations.

Machine Selection

This is a part of game selection, because often machines and their games can be one and the same. However, there are many machines that have more than one game, such as multi-game video slots. Other times, even simple single-game video slots may have different versions. These games may look the same as the ones you have decided to select, but may not be. The easiest example is among video slots games where two identical looking machines can have extremely different pay and play programs. Such subtle differences can easily be seen in video poker games, and also in some reel slot games, but are cleverly hidden in many video slot games. Some of the video reel slots have so many pays, and combinations of pays and bonuses, that it becomes very difficult to find out exactly how these games may be different from each other. The easiest clue I can give you is to look at the top jackpot amount. For example, many of these games will show the top jackpot as 25,000 coins. An identical looking machine, elsewhere in the same casino, or perhaps in another casino, may show that very same jackpot as 12,500 coins. Big difference. What does this mean? It means you are getting less for the same risk at the game that only offers the 12,500 coins jackpot, all other items being equal. Often when you see this you will also notice that the other pays on the machine don't pay exactly as much, or in the same manner, as the machine with the bigger jackpot. Usually, these differences in the top jackpot amounts are a good indicator that the game is just a bit different, in some ways. The most glaring of these ways is, of course, the difference in the top award, but, many times you will find that the winning combinations among the remaining pays aren't paying the same as the other game, even when everything looks the same. Often the difference may be as simple as the game paying only left to right, while the other, better, game paid both ways. Or, this game may be only a 5-line game, while the other was a 9-line game. Perhaps the bonus entry structure is less frequent because the requirements aren't set to occur as often as in the other game. Or, some of the pay symbols, or bonus awards or rounds, may be missing.

There are a host of such subtle differences among these games, so it is important that your machine selection also includes comparisons. This will require a little legwork on your part and some skills in observation. Among the video slots you will have to do some investigating. You will need to read the help and pay screens, learn the payoff and bonuses structure—and the amounts—and then compare these to other machines of their kind, and especially to other machines that look the same. You can usually save yourself some time by first looking at the top jackpot amounts, which should give you an indication of the differences in the machine's pay and bonus structure. But there will be no substitute for your diligence and your ability to apply the skills and knowledge you have acquired. Your success as a video slot player will directly depend on your abilities to do these things. The best hint I can give you is to check out the video slots I have listed in this book, as well as those I also mentioned in my earlier Slots book. These are among the best there is, and therefore your game and machine selections should be that much easier.

Brand Name Selection

This is closely tied in with the above item. Machine and game selections are often influenced by the *manufacturer* of the game and machine. It's the same sort of principle as that with which you may be familiar from just shopping at the market or discount store. Among slot machines, this is similarly so. There are some very well established "brand names" among manufacturers of video slot machines. In this book, I have identified those I consider to be the best, and therefore the standard by which you can judge any video slot machine, its performance, its pay program, and its potential for profitable play. One of the "secrets" of successful play is the acquisition of knowledge regarding the machine's manufacturer and familiarity with their products. Begin your machine and game selection by first identifying the brand names of the machines and games. Once you have done that, you will gain the standard by which to compare the other available games on the casino floor. There will be many machines and many games. Some of them will look the same, or be very similar to the "brand name," but may not play or pay quite as well. By simply being able to recognize the brand name of the machine or game, you will be well under way toward making intelligent and informed decisions.

Game Detail Selection

All of these items concerning selection are intertwined at many levels. Game detail selection refers to the small nuances in the game, and the often hard-to-see differences in pays, or in the way the games play. For video slots, this is a little more complicated. Here the game detail selection is a precise science. Your abilities in this area directly influence your odds of success when playing these machines. It is imperative that you first learn everything about any video slot machine, or game, you are contemplating playing. The machines offer this information among their pay, play, and help screens. Take the time to read all of this, and to understand it. Don't start playing until you know what pays what, and under what circumstances, how it is done, what needs to be activated to do this, how many coins must be played to get the best payoffs and bonuses, and so on. Also important is to find out whether this is a "doubler" machine, or a "buy-a-pay" machine. These are all the "details" in your game selection. I can again give you a hint by referring you to the machines and games I have selected in this book, and in my other books. If you simply focus on those, you will be far ahead of many other players who will not know this and will therefore be dancing in the dark, hoping to catch the right game and the right time. You can do better, because you already have most of this knowledge.

Size of the Wager Selection

This is a companion to the game detail selection. Once you have identified the details of what this machine is, and how it plays and pays, your next step is to decide how much you will invest. This is part of your bankroll decisions, but in this case we assume you have already settled on your bankroll for this game, and now are simply judging how much to invest, and how many coins, or lines, you will play. Among video slots, this selection principle is more complicated. First, you must learn the details, as shown earlier. Once you have done this, and now understand exactly what this machine is, and how it plays and pays, then you can decide how many coins you intend to play. Your first decision should be regarding the number of available paylines. If the machine has five lines, then the absolute minimum must be five coins. If it has nine lines, then this is nine coins. And so on. This should be automatic for any such video reel slot machine. *None* of these should be played with any *less* than the minimum *one coin per payline*. At least. Without this absolutely minimum action, you will be a loser no matter what you have learned, and if you have even thought about playing such video slots for any less than this absolute minimum, you have not learned very much. Yet. But you will. You will learn this two ways. One is the easy way, and that is to follow this advice, from the information gained here. The other is to play this way and realize that you have won, but didn't get paid because you didn't play at least that minimum of one coin per payline. Once you do this, you won't ever forget it, and it will haunt you the rest of your life. Consequently, it is essential that whenever you play any of the multi-line video slots, you play *at the very least* the minimum one coin *per payline* to activate *all* the paylines. However, your decisions do not end there. In addition, you should determine whether you should play the *maximum* coins, or not. This will depend on the other information about the machine and the game, as I have already listed earlier, or will discuss below. All of this information becomes necessary when you make a decision that will cost you money.

As a general rule, *none* of these video slots machines should *ever be played for less than the maximum coins allowed*. This is because on most of these machines you "buy-a-pay," and therefore if you play any less than the maximum bet you will not get the best bonuses, the best pays, the jackpots, and will not get the best payback percentage of which such a machine is capable by its play program. If you still aren't sure about this, do what I do— *always play maximum coins.* If you can't afford to play maximum coins, *don't play* until you *can* afford to do so. Otherwise, you are throwing your money away because you will never force the casino to pay you the amounts to which you are entitled by the machine's pay program. In all honesty, this should be automatic, and your decision already made up. However, there are times when skilled decisions can make a difference, but to do so you must actually be very skilled and knowledgeable about the game. In the end, that will be your decision, based on the abilities and skills you acquire through the information in this book and your own abilities and playing successes. Nevertheless, I will try one more time to stress the importance of playing maximum coins, no matter how big a wager that may be. Just remember this—if you don't play maximum coins or credits per spin on all available paylines, you will *never* get the maximum payback of which that machine is capable. You will also *never win the top award.* It's that simple.

Payout Hierarchy Selection

This continues from the above. Your wager selection will be influenced by the payout hierarchy. This is the part on the machines that shows the graduated scale of payments and bonuses offered. This information is usually found under the Pays menu icon, and it tells you not only what amounts the game pays, but also how and when, and with what combinations. Further, it shows you whether this is a "doubler" or a "buy-a-pay" machine, or game. Also, some of these machines, and games, may look the same but have different payout hierarchy. This we have already discussed. Therefore, it is also very important that you don't just *look* at this payout hierarchy, but also *understand* what it means and how it will affect your bankroll, your play and session investment, and your win expectation. You acquire this understanding by combining all of the information shown here, and applying it to your *overall* machine, or game, selection.

Play Methodology Selection

This has a lot to do with the kind of playing strategy, and discipline, which you will employ in your gaming. Learning information and acquiring the abilities and skills required to properly apply that information to your playing success, are all necessary prerequisites. Eventually, you will have to also include a playing strategy, often referred to as the "overall methodology," meaning the approach you take to your play. Selecting the correct play methodology is tricky. Not all methods, often called "systems," are appropriate for all machines, games, or occasions. Much depends on your bankroll, and on your win goals. The best way to approach the selection of any methodology of play is to first decide what kind of a machine or game you will be playing, the amount of your bankroll, and the number and frequency of your playing sessions. Once you have decided this, then you can search through available strategies to determine the best one to use for this specific occasion. A little later in this book I will present some of the simplest and most easily applied strategies for profitable play. This does not mean that you cannot use your own strategy, or those which you may have learned elsewhere. Many of these strategies contain strong and applicable methodology, as it applies to particular games, or machine situations. In the end, the decision will be yours. For now, the methods I offer here will empower you to start playing immediately, and, later, to enhance your play according to your abilities and growing skills.

Size of Bankroll Selection

This is again dependent on a number of factors. Simply put, the best way to gauge the size of your playing bankroll is to determine how much of your money you can afford to risk, without its loss having an adverse effect on your ability to continue living at your present rate of comfort and reality. If you think that a loss of $500 won't affect your ability to pay the rent, the mortgage, or the power bills, then this is the bankroll you should take, and modify your play, and win goals, accordingly. For higher amounts, this will directly depend on the value of that money to you at the time you are making this determination.

Never play slots, or any gambling game, with money you cannot afford to lose!

If you do this just once, you will think it's okay to do it again, and it's never okay to do this. Doing this, and playing this way and with this money, means you are using "scared" money, the total loss of which will very adversely affect you, your family, and your life. This is a prescription for disaster. Individually, for each machine or game you select, the size of your bankroll should be called your *session* bankroll. This is the part of your overall bankroll that you will allocate to this one machine, or game, on *this* particular playing session, this one time. Such an allocation should reflect the overall size of your casino bankroll, divided into the session stakes according to the game of your choice, the time you wish to play, and the win goals you desire to achieve.

Play Duration Selection

Similarly to the bankroll selection, the duration of your play on that particular machine, or game, should be governed by the amount of money you have allocated to this session and your ability to physically sustain the play effort. If you get bored, stop. Being bored means you have lost interest in this game, and if you keep playing you will waste your money and your time because you will not play the game correctly and will easily lose sight of your win goals. It's a trap. Be aware of it. Playing can often get boring, especially when you play for several hours at a time. If your attention span is short, and you tire easily, or feel upset, or gain any kind of a negative emotion, then plan your play duration in short bursts. How short? Well, that depends on you. I can sit at a video slot machine for hours on end and never get bored, as long as I have the starting mind-set that I have a certain goal, and that includes the time at the game. Other times, I decide that short sessions will be better because my personal psyche at that moment demands quick bursts to sustain the interest. We all are different, and you will need to choose according to your own particular situation, personally, financially, psychologically, and emotionally.

Never play any video slot machine past the point where it continues to interest you.

If you have properly identified your goals and win objectives, then you should be psychologically prepared for as long as it takes, under the circumstances of your available casino time. If at any time you lose this conviction, and you lose interest in the game, that is a warning sign. Your mind and body are telling you that you have set goals outside of your ability, either mentally or physically. Listen to these hints. They will save you money. Therefore, your time at the game selection requires you to also be honest with yourself, and not set periods of time at play that you can't handle. If you don't know you have these limitations, and you find that out while playing, listen to what your mind and body are telling you. Many people don't realize that they have such limitations. They get overly excited in the casino and then lose perspective on themselves and their lives, which mostly means they lose their money as well. Once in a casino, maintain your rational approach to your play. Remember that any activity requires mental and physical exertion. Playing video slots is no different. It will take time, effort, and concentration. Once you lose any of these three, or start to feel not quite committed, stop. Take a break. Go eat. Go take a swim, a spa, a massage. Sleep. Sit in the lounge. See a show. Whatever. You may only need a very short break, such as merely a few minutes. When I start to feel this way, I go to the restroom, wash my face, walk around the casino, maybe walk outside for a few breaths of fresh air, and I'm set to go again, refreshed and able to concentrate. This is very important. After you have been to a casino a few times, and practiced this advice, you will easily see just how important it is to your gaming success. Don't let your play of the machine control you. *You* control your time at this play. The game will reward you for it.

When to Play Selection

This will be affected by your general lifestyle. Most people get up in the morning to go to work at 9:00 A.M., and come back after 5:00 P.M., then have dinner, and so on, go to bed. This dictates the kind of lifestyle they lead. At the casino most people entirely forget this and start to act as if there were no need to sleep, rest, or do anything other than indulge in total abandonment. That is okay, believe me. There's nothing better than to become that free. For a while, that is, and hopefully without losing your head, and your money, while doing it. Unfortunately, many people get so wrapped up in this sudden freedom that they forget their rational mind. That is bad. If you want to have this "mad time," it is perfectly okay to do so. Just be aware that it will cost you money and that it can cost you your well-made plans as well. Once you interrupt your routine, you will become trapped in paradise and can easily lose sight of even the most basic human reasoning. If this happens to you, you are lost, at least for the duration of this trip. But fear not. It can be overcome.

When you plan your trip to the casino, regardless of whether you live next door, or have to plan a vacation to fly or drive there, also realize that you will become enthusiastically enthralled in the experience. Plan for it. Plan for the "mad time," and that way you will be able to allocate time, resources, energy, and bankroll to these experiences. You will then realize that's part of your casino plan and will have a great time enjoying it. Then, when you tire yourself out, remind yourself that it's time to get rest, regain your composure and reason, because now it will be time to go and play to win. Playing to win requires a clear head and a rested body. You need to make some adjustments to your "normal" lifestyle and life's schedule. Playing video slots to win may require you to play at odd hours, because that's when the pickin's are good. For example, most people tend to crowd around the video slots at dinner time and just after. Bad time. Everyone plays then, and the selections are few and far between. If possible, play either very late at night, such as after midnight, or very early in the morning, such as from about 5:00 A.M. The best time to play these machines is usually from about 2:00 A.M. until about 9:00 A.M. This is the time in between the end of the rush from the night before and prior to the rush from the "normal" morning risers, who play before and after breakfast.

There are very good reasons for this kind of play.

First, there will be fewer players. You will have better

choices among the machines, and therefore you'll be able to make better selections. You will also get better service from the employees, because there are fewer people for them to look after.

Second, the machines you will select are quite likely to have been given a lot of play the night before and therefore will be more primed for your skilled selections and play.

If you want to do this and can handle it physically, stay up for some hours during the busy times the night before and watch the machines you think you will want to play. Don't play, just watch. See which machines get the heaviest play and what, if anything, they have paid out. This kind of research can serve you well when you rise early the next morning and go hit the machines before the day crowd hustles in. Of course, you may want to go to bed early so you *can* get up early. Fine. You can still get the information you want by asking the employees. They may not know for sure, because they have just come on duty after the swing shift leaves at 2:00 A.M., but I can assure you that if there was any kind of a significant win on the previous shift, these people in that same area will have heard about it. Although this is nothing more than simple empirical research, and is only useful as a guideline, and just one more piece in the overall informational supply, it provides a good gauge by which to modify your game selections. As a general rule of thumb, try to play video slots whenever other people are *not* playing. Stay away from crowds and times when machines are crowded. That's the time to watch and learn and remember.

Casinos Where to Play and What Kinds of Machines to Play There Selection

A long title, but pertinent. Which casinos to play in? Well, if you live near one, or two, and that's it, then your choices are simple, provided these are the casinos you wish to visit. As a general rule of thumb, in the United States the best casinos are in Las Vegas, Nevada. Machines in the State of Nevada are usually much better than any other state, while those in Las Vegas are the best of any slots anywhere. On the East Coast, machines in Connecticut are better than machines in Atlantic City. If you want to know which casinos in the Midwest offer the better games—and yes, there are casinos even in the Midwest that have some very good video slots—I refer you to the *Midwest Gaming and Travel* magazine, published in Waseca, Minnesota. You can look it up on the Web, under the same name, all together, lowercase characters, and then the dot-com, of course. But overall, nothing can beat the video slots in Las Vegas. They are the best, loosest machines anywhere. Also the best variety of video slots is found there, as well as most of the newest games.

DISCIPLINE

Of all the Keys to Winning, this one sounds the simplest, but is the hardest of them all. We all understand the value of discipline, especially when it comes to our money. This is accentuated when we talk about the casino environment. Everything in the casino is designed to separate us from any sense of reality. The casinos are a wondrous land, where everything seems possible as long as you still have money. The money is the lifeblood of all of this excitement. Without it, you are nothing more than dead wood, and you will be flushed out in a hurry. Having discipline as part of your winning objectives saves you from the inglorious fate of being washed clean, hung out to dry, and tossed away as yet another of the ill prepared and unwary. Having discipline as part of your tricks of the trade when you go gambling simply means to make the commitment to play wisely, with reason, with goals in mind. It means playing with all of the empowering Keys to Winning, as well as all the other information I have shared here. If you want to have your "mad time," that's okay too. Budget for it, realize it, recognize it, place it as part of your overall game plan. Even that will then become part of your discipline, as long as you don't let the thrill of this overwhelm you and allow it to completely drown all your plans, and your discipline along with it.

Unfortunately, *making* a commitment to self-discipline when going to the casino is very easy. *Keeping to it* once you get to the casino is very hard. So hard, in fact, that the vast majority of people who arrive at the casino completely convinced they will not allow this experience to get the better of them do just that. They let it get the better of them. And fast. You'd be surprised. Very often as soon as these people walk through the door. Suddenly, they see all the excitement, all the games, all the flashing lights, the sounds of money and chips—the entire atmosphere captures them. In the door they go, and out the door go all of their well-meaning and carefully conceived plans. Also their sense of discipline, and mostly all their other senses as well. It happens to just about everyone, even hardened veterans of the casino lifestyle. All of us are human beings, and we are not perfect. We have failures, and the lack of discipline is the greatest failure of us all. We see it everywhere around us. To offer the easiest guideline, discipline in gambling simply means to remain conscious of the value of your money and conscious of your desired goals and objectives. It means, mostly, to not allow yourself to be drawn into the very comfortable, but financially deadly, sense of "Why not? it's only money" syndrome. Once you have experienced the casino lifestyle a few times, you will often hear many people say things like that. These people are trapped in the losses they have incurred and are now trying to rationalize it for themselves. They don't actually expect anyone else to listen to them, or to really understand what expressions such as this really mean. They have just resigned themselves to the loss of all their money and to the "I no longer care" attitude. That's the danger sign. Once you stop caring about the value of the money you are using to play—or are winning—then you have lost the discipline that comes with realizing this money isn't just coins, tokens, or gaming chips. This money actually spends, like in buying food, gas for your car, and paying bills. It is real money; it has real meaning. Discipline really means to remember this, and play accordingly.

This doesn't mean that you must be, or should be, a miser. Playing too carefully is also a prescription for disaster. I have already mentioned that "scared" money flies away quickly. Don't play that way. To win, you must play aggressively and with a sufficient bankroll to justify your level of action. All of this is covered in the other Keys to Winning. Discipline is the glue that holds it all together. Once the glue stops holding, it all falls apart.

WIN GOAL

What is a win goal? In simplest terms, a win goal is the realistic expectation of a certain win amount, based on the potential of available wins relative to the bankroll allowed, session stake allocated, expertise at the game, plus time at the game. This simple formula will equal your end-result profitability, in winning situations, and end-result saving of money that would have been lost in negative situations. For example, most gamblers will say that a 2 percent win goal over and above the session stake is a very great achievement. The casino, for example, has a win goal of around 2 percent for most blackjack games, around an average of 4 percent for slots, and about 20 percent over all the games they offer. Some games will make them more money because people will play them badly. Although basic blackjack, for example, can be played to less than 0.5 percent casino advantage, most players will play the game so badly that the casinos actually yield anywhere from 2 to 6 percent, and often even more, on a game that can actually yield a *player* advantage—if played properly and with skill (for more information on blackjack, I refer you to my book *Powerful Profits from Blackjack*).

For video slots, the average expectation is around 5 percent to perhaps 12 percent, depending on the casino, where it is located, and what the competition is like. In Las Vegas, the casinos mostly count on around 8 percent as their *average* win goal for all of their video slots combined. Sometimes more, sometimes less, but overall around this figure. The reality is, however, that all the slots combined—reel and video—will pay the casino much more. Overall, the casinos will get about 80 percent of all their revenue from slots, and their average win-goal expectation over all their machines turns out to be around 12 percent, and sometimes more. The reason is, primarily, that even video slot players play so badly. They choose machines that don't offer the best value, or machines that offer low payoffs and low payback programs, and generally play like silly cattle blindly bringing their money as offerings to these machine idols. The difference between the casino and the player is that the casino can easily have a much lower win goal, because their doors are open 24/7/365. Their games make money all the time, every hour, every day, every week, every month, every year, without ever needing a rest or a break. Human players can't play like that. While the casino can easily offer a game where it can reasonably expect only less than 1 percent profit, it will get this all the time, always, over the short term as well as the long haul. You, the player, can't play like that. Therefore, whenever gamblers say to me that they expect a 2 percent return and consider this as good, I politely tell them that's great, and quietly chuckle. These "gamblers" are trying to play like the casino, trying to beat the casino at their own game of survival. Trying to "outlast" the overall game percentages. This will result in nothing more than the gambler's eventual ruin and a whole lot of frustration in between. Gamblers in general, and video slot players in particular, must have win goals not only commensurate with their bankroll, session stakes, and so on, as listed earlier, but also the realization that their exposure to the game will only be a very short slice of the game's overall event reality. Therefore, such win goals cannot—and should not—be measured in percentages relative to the way that the casinos figure their own odds and win goals. Rather, these win goals should be measured in terms of what the game *can yield*, especially if played correctly, and if selected in accordance with the various selection criteria I listed. It is also important at this point to introduce a derivative of the win-goal criterion, called the win expectation.

The win goal is what you have set as your desired objective, realistically based on the various principles already amply demonstrated. The win *expectation*, however, is based within the reality of the game itself and, most specifically, in that very short-term slice of that one specific game's event experience. The point is that throughout your casino visit no playing session is ever independent of your other sessions. All your video slot–playing sessions are *combined together* to reveal, in the end as you go home, the *entire block* of all sessions combined. Whatever results you have achieved at that point determine your average per session win-expectation percentage, and your win-goal achievement levels. This information can then be used by you to more accurately reflect how well you played, and to modify your goals and expectations for future visits. But you must take *everything* into account, even the value of all the additions you have earned, such as your comps and freebies, and club points. All of this combines to affect your goals, expectations, and final relative results.

This brings us to the final item in this chapter, and that is the overall win goals and overall win expectation. This is set by you based on bankroll, skill, and other abilities, as stated here in this book, as well as whatever other information and skills you may have acquired. If you have understood what I have attempted to illustrate, then your total win goal for your casino visit should be directly relative to your bankroll, and comfort level at the games, as well as your other gaming and playing skills, including selection skills. As a guide, your overall win *goal* should be to double your bankroll. Your win *expectation* should be to come home with 20 percent over and above your bring-in bankroll. If you achieve anything close to this, then you have just beaten the casino, and the video slot machines. You have done what less than 1 percent of all casino players are able to do! You have become a good, knowledgeable, and responsible player. Congratulations!

8

The *EZ Pay*™ Ticket System

This new technology makes playing slots in various denominations possible. Also known as the ticket-in, ticket-out system, or TITO for short, this great new option on IGT machines and games allows you to cash out without having to haul all those buckets of coins, wait for endless coin fills, and have the annoyance of the machine locking up for each $50 in pays, as was the case on most nickel and lower-denomination machines for many years. It also allows you portability, because the tickets can be used as cash and can be inserted into other machines that also have this ticketing system. This means that you no longer have to cash out and buy in again. You can use only these tickets, and move from machine to machine more easily. Furthermore, if you are playing any kind of a session-based slot method, you can use these tickets to keep track of where you are in your session play and how well you are doing. Using these tickets becomes very important in your continued session accounting, and having them easily available makes it simpler for you to employ the slot-playing strategies of your choice.

There are several competing systems that are similar, but this particular IGT system is by far the best and easiest for you to play. It works with all of the games I have shown in this book, and for that reason alone I recommend it as one of the features you should look for in your selection of machines and games. It will allow you to manage your play time and bankroll a lot better, and with greater ease and efficiency. It will also allow you to change denominations on the machines you select to play, and therefore have much greater control over the amounts of money you are spending. These tickets and this system allow you greater control over your winnings, as well as making it easy to account for where you are in your win goals and objectives. Finally, these tickets are easily carried, stored on your person, and kept in wallets and purses. They are as good as cash, but not nearly as bulky or as obvious. This makes it very much more secure, and better for your play in all respects. The *EZ Pay*™ Ticket System is IGT's premier solution for reducing or eliminating hopper fills, simplifying hand pays, promoting selectable-denomination gaming, and ultimately increasing playtime and customer service—resulting in much greater convenience for the players.

Using the *EZ Pay*™ Ticket System, players experience little or no hassle. The *EZ*™ *Pay* Ticket System is an independent system linking *EZ Play*™ gaming machines that print and read cash-out tickets. Up to 50 *EZ Play*™ gaming machines can be linked together in a loop, and numerous loops can be linked using IGT's innovative cross-validation technology. Equipped with thermal ticket printers and advanced bill validators, *EZ Play*™ gaming machines allow greater flexibility for controlling slot operations. By combining ticket printers with traditional hopper pays, casinos can now program machines to pay a portion of each cashout in coins—with the balance paid in the form of a printed ticket—or set the machine to pay out printed tickets only, using the hopper solely as a backup.

From a player's perspective, tickets act just like cash. A cash-out ticket from one *EZ Play*™ machine can be inserted into the bill validator of any other *EZ Play*™ machine on the system, instantly transferring credits from one machine to another. *EZ Pay*™ tickets can also be exchanged for cash at a cashier's station, redeemed by automated ticket redemption devices, cashed on the casino floor by attendants using wireless validation units, or held by the player for use at a later time. The *EZ Pay*™ system also supports the innovative multi-denomination features of popular multi-line, multi-hand game themes, thereby eliminating the players' frustration in searching for their favorite games in the right denomination. Players simply insert bills, coins, or tickets into their favorite game and select their preferred wager denomination—from 1 cent up to $25—to initiate play. With multi-denomination wagers available on a single machine, the *EZ Pay*™ system also enables "last penny play," eliminating the hassle players endure—cashing out, collecting, and converting coins—when a denomination change requires moving to a new machine.

EZ PAY™ TICKET SYSTEM FEATURES

The *EZ Pay*™ Ticket System, the premier software solution for managing ticket-in, ticket-out slot operations, contains features that answer the demand for operational efficiencies and improved customer service. IGT's *EZ Play*™ gaming machines allow the casino to divide a machine's cash-out between the hopper and the *EZ Pay*™ ticket printer. IGT's Game King™, Game King Plus™, S2000™, and Vision Series *EZ Play*™ machines combine the latest advances in ticket printing and redemption hardware with the following:

- Multi-denomination software
- The world's largest, most successful game library
- Dazzling glass graphics
- The best cabinet designs in the industry
- Unparalleled functionality, flexibility, and security

The *EZ Pay*™ system also supports federal guidelines for jackpot reporting. Jackpot or cash-out amounts exceeding the single win limit set on *EZ Play*™ machines cause the game to lock while a hand pay request is recorded with the *EZ Pay*™ system. When the game is reset, the machine's ticket printer provides a receipt for the payout amount. Wireless validation terminals running on handheld devices also expand the convenience of the *EZ Pay*™ Ticket System. Properly equipped floor attendants can validate tickets with the handheld scanner, print receipts from belt-mounted receipt printers, and pay customers right on the floor from any corner of the casino—the entire process secured by complex data encryption. Automated ticket redemption devices provide an easy and convenient way for you to redeem cashout tickets issued by *EZ Play*™ machines right on the casino floor. Valid tickets redeemed through an *EZ Pay*™ Ticket System redemption station are paid on the spot by highsecurity, electronically controlled coin and currency hoppers. Interactive touchscreen cashier workstations accept data entries, process system commands, and communicate important system status and ticket validation information at the touch of a screen icon. These easy-to-use touchscreen graphical icons guide users through the ticket validation process, using bar-code scanners or manual data entry. The *EZ Pay*™ system also allows players to exchange cash for tickets of equal value printed at a cashier station's secure ticket printer. These "purchase tickets" provide a fast, easy way for players to place credits on their favorite *EZ Play*™ machines.

EZ Pay™ promotional tickets can also be used by casinos to reward valuable customers and can be created in batches that can be mailed out, or printed on the spot for a personal touch. With custom ticket categories, date/time ranges, and detailed accounting reports, *EZ Pay*™ promotional tickets allow casinos to establish and monitor the free-credit game play on *EZ Play*™ gaming machines. If you are one of the lucky people who gets these promotional tickets, either in the mail or in the casino, you will now be able to use them immediately, without further validation, on any of the designated machines and games. Saves you time standing in line at the club booth or the promotional center. Nice!

The *EZ Pay*™ accounting functions control the auditing and communication of all ticket and event information in the *EZ Pay*™ system. From slot floor, cashier station, and soft-count drop activities through archiving and exporting ticket data to a central accounting system, the *EZ Pay*™ system is the premier software solution to manage ticket-in, ticket-out slot operations. Since IGT *EZ Pay*™ tickets are the same size as U.S. currency, existing bill sorters can count, sort, and separate tickets from currency during the soft-count process. Using an *EZ Pay*™ soft-count touchscreen workstation, operators can control a manual bar-code scanner or an automated high-speed scanner to reconcile *EZ Pay*™ tickets to tickets scanned during the drop process, view soft count logs, and create detailed soft count reports. *EZ Pay*™ audit processes allow for the validation of torn, damaged, or defaced tickets, controlling the balancing and adjustment of cashier and soft-count sessions, and providing a variety of status and reconciliation reports. A sample of *EZ Pay*™ reports include:

- Session reconciliation and audit reports
- Ticket issuance, liability, and redemption reports
- Expired, void, and jackpot ticket reports

- Cashier session and cashier ticket issuance reports
- Promotion detail and performance reports
- Soft count with verification, exception, and expected drop reports
- Gross, missing, exception, and unexpected meter reports
- Missed can and ticket drop variance reports
- User access security, workstation, and CC (Counting Control) configuration reports

The *EZ Pay*™ Ticket System also collects machine meter data from every machine connected to the system for reconciliation with audit and soft-count sessions. Meter data includes cash-out tickets issued and dropped, promotional tickets issued and dropped, and traditional coin and currency meter data. Communication between the *EZ Pay*™ Ticket System and most casino management systems provides for audit, soft count, and cashier cage accounting for improved slot operations as well as the ticket reporting functionality required by the local jurisdiction. The *EZ Pay*™ Ticket System architecture has many forward-thinking features, including the reliable Windows®2000 operating system and SQL Server™ 2000 database technology. The *EZ Pay*™ Ticket System continues to improve with the addition of PromoPAK™ Module functionality for creating and printing customized promo tickets and purchase tickets. Using the new GSA standard protocol SAS 6.00 capabilities, the promo ticket feature gives the casino's marketing department the ability to create custom batches of *EZ Pay*™ tickets for promotional tickets for promotional credit game play on advanced funds transfer (AFT)–ready *EZ Play*™ gaming machines. You can make your smart play work to your advantage by using these promotional offers wisely. The casinos can set a ticket type to control how category members play and convert a promotion's tickets, as follows:

- Non-cashable: only accumulated winnings or regular credits are redeemable.
- Cashable: the promo tickets and residual promotional credits can be redeemed for cash.
- Use an instantly recognizable 25-character name for tickets' printed title.
- Gather related promotions into customizable categories such as:
  - Demographic segment
  - Regional locality
  - Event series
- Marketing method use *EZ Pay*™'s Promotion Pay Performance and Promotion Detail report features to evaluate promotions by:
  - Category
  - Ticket type
  - Machine
  - Hourly play

Establish the credit amount printed on each of the promotion's tickets.

- Each ticket by batch displays:
  - Promotion title and name
  - Cashable/non-cashable
  - Effective dates
  - Promotional credit value
- Create and print multiple ticket batches for the promotion.
- Control the validation cycle of each ticket batch by setting or staggering:
  - Effective play days from print date
  - Play hours during valid day
  - Days of the week selected for play
- Determine the number of tickets the batch prints
- Further restrict the cash-out of residual promotional credits

- Assign date range for producing batches of a promotion's tickets

To control purchase ticket production, *EZ Pay*™ cashiers may only print one purchase ticket at a time under their open validation session. A special ticket printer connected directly to a cashier's workstation prints each purchase ticket while a receipt of the purchase ticket transaction prints on a receipt printer for the cashier's record. Although the *EZ Pay*™ Ticket System operates independently, ticket data of interest may be exported to a central accounting system. Many standard *EZ Pay*™ reports allow casinos to track, audit, and account for all Promo Tickets and Purchase Tickets produced along with regular machine cash-out tickets. Now you have a fast, easy way to place credits on your favorite *EZ Play*™ machines with the *EZ Pay*™ Purchase Ticket feature. This feature allows you to purchase tickets at a cashier's workstation that are redeemable at *EZ Play*™ machines or other cashier stations. Accessible within a cashier's open validation session, the Purchase Ticket feature provides a unique number and a printed receipt for the cashier's reconciliation record. Further, the *EZ Pay*™ system provides both the players and the employees with a safe and secure way to reduce the coin and currency-handling burden. It also improves coinless efficiency by encouraging players to:

- Exchange cash and coin for purchase tickets.
- Receive slot marker purchase tickets instead of tokens.
- Establish user privileges that allow purchase tickets over the maximum amount to be printed with appropriate override approval.
- Click a Quick Selection button to quickly print a purchase ticket for one of the displayed preset amounts.
- Create promotions that reward purchase ticket trans-

actions while boosting coinless play—like giving a $1 Promo Ticket free for each $10 Purchase Ticket.

As more video slots take over more spaces on the casino slot floor, these ticketing systems will become more important to your successful slot play. While I realize that a lot of the information I have presented here may sound technical, I wanted you to be among the very first—and thus far only— readers of a book about slots that tells you the whole story behind these ticketing systems. Knowing the inner workings of how casinos do business, and how these systems affect them, provides you with more knowledge than other players, leading to better success and better decisions. A TITO system is one of those technological innovations that are already part of the modern casino slot floor of the twenty-first century. As you go from casino to casino looking for the best video slots that are available—don't forget to look for this IGT *EZ Pay*™ Ticketing System as part of the machine or game. It will give you greater flexibility in your gaming and provide you with the easiest and most portable options for making your strategy play count.

Strategies for Video Slots

Most people think that there are no strategies for slot machines, whether they are reel slots or the new video slots. In fact, many experts contend that there can never be any winning strategy for slots at all. This is because—so they say—slots are a negative expectation game and, therefore, the machine's program will always assure the players of a loss over the long term and thus always assure the casino of a win. These experts are mostly those whose perspective on all casino games is firmly vested in mathematics and probabilities. Each time they are challenged regarding this view, they quickly grab the nearest math book and like a zealous old-time preacher hold it reverently and pound on it, citing the phrases and chants of the statisticians and probability theorists as if reciting holy gospel. To them, everything in the universe revolves around mathematics, and nothing else has any truth to it. In accordance with that dogma, casino games with an in-built house edge are negative expectation games from the player's perspective and, therefore, the players cannot ever win and will never win on such games over the long haul. There are many such experts and many books filled with these theories of limitations.

The main problem with this kind of thinking is that the purveyors of such opinions are themselves deluded by the so-presumed scientific discipline they consider to be the one and only window into the truths of the universe. As a result, they are locked inside a box and they don't know it; anyone or anything that even postulates the possibility of something outside of that box is a heretic to be burned at the academic stake. Yet, their own assertions prove them wrong— or only partially correct. They don't allow for the possibility of something else being the truth and, consequently, no discussion with them is possible.

The only viable means of showing them the possibility of something else is to point out their own words and how oddly inappropriate they are. The key words in all such mathematically based strategies for casino games, particularly those that are mathematically negative expectation games for the players, are the words "long term" and "long haul." Both are favorite expressions in the arsenal of math experts who are trying to quantify and create strategies for casino games. Such mathematically based strategies can work quite well when applied to games such as blackjack, some video poker games, and to live poker, because these are not fixed negative expectation games for their players. These games can be turned into player positive expectation games by skill, and therefore mathematically based and math-derived strategies have a place in the knowledge and skills that apply to these games. They are also much more statistically definable, which makes them perfect for such quantification and their thus-derived math-based strategies. So far so good. The problem begins to rear its ugly head when these math gurus try to apply the same principles and standards to what are, mathematically, player negative expectation games, such as roulette, baccarat, craps, and slots. Here the methodology fails, so the math people say that no play-ers can ever win on such games. But—players *do* win on these games, and win often. To reconcile this with their the-ories, the math experts cite those two now famous expres-sions I mentioned just a short while ago: "long term" and "long haul." Now we come to the crux of the matter.

By the very principles of their own mathematics, such theories and therein-based strategies for casino games have to allow for the possibility of infinite events, and, therefore, extract their principles and numbers from such protracted sequences. Although the generally accepted sampling has become 10 million events, this is far from sufficient to allow for the extension of the actual probability theory. Such a theory must, by its very nature, be infinite. Otherwise there would be no way to determine whether or not the sampling events were, or were not, a simple anomaly, or if they actu-ally were the true representation of the eventual parity of events. Any strategy for casino games must postulate the long term and the long haul, because otherwise it wouldn't work out as nicely as the mathematicians expect. The world would not be nice and neat within that box of numbers.

But the truth is that the world is *not* nice and neat—it is chaotic, and mathematics has little or no value in it. Quan-tum mechanics proves the unreliability of macro-models of general relativity, and the unified field theory has therefore been proposed as a reconciliation between what is essen-tially random chaos at the micro-universal level and what appears to be law-related order of the macro-universe. This simply means that what we think we see and know are in actuality realities nothing like what they appear. The apparent "order" of the universe is nothing of the sort, and, therefore, the apparent "order" of mathematics as a means of under-standing it is nothing of the sort. Using mathematically based and derived strategies for casino games is simply an arbitrary model, vested in a narrow misunderstanding of the realities of universal events and the truth of the very fabric upon which it is created and founded. It is a misunderstanding of these principles inasmuch as the expressions "long term" and "long haul" mean nothing to the day you will be playing the slots, and similarly mean nothing to the infinite model of the universe, even if we allow for the apparent order of the general relativity model.

Even under such macro-views, the eventual parity of events may take billions of years, or even longer in the span of universal statistics. Then, and only then, will we be able to make a determination as to the possible validity of such events and their possibly applicable meaning to gambling strategies. At the same time, the micro-universe of quantum mechanics clearly shows that chaos is the order of the foundation, where effects precede their causes and time and space are interchangeably nonlinear. The Super String Theory of quantum mechanics,* recently proposed again as the unified field theory, offers a reconciliation with general relativity and preserves parity of events in mathematical law, but only under the requisite postulation of several additional dimensions, all of which make even this theory still highly subject to conjecture. What all of this inevitably means is that even expressions such as "long term" and "long haul" are at best only indicative, and at worst only labels upon jars the content of which we don't know.

It all boils down to the simple truth that all casino games can be beaten, and that players will win, and do win, even on casino games that these mathematical theorists conclude are player negative expectation games. The simple truth is that nothing in nature, and certainly nothing made by man, can ever be perfect. This goes for gambling theories as well, and particularly for mathematically de-

The Elegant Universe, Brian Greene, Vintage, February 2000.

rived strategies, because those work only on those games whose statistical parity of events can be readily and immediately seen within the very short term of the human observation, such as through a deck of cards in blackjack, the payback program for video poker machines, and a hand of cards in live poker. All these are easily understood and easily quantified events, and their parity of relative occurrences happen quickly, and immediately, easily within the grasp of the human's ability to notice this in the immediacy of the game at hand. All the other games require an understanding far beyond that employed for these more immediately understood situations, and as a result they aren't so nicely enumerated, or so easily used within those same math models. As a direct consequence, math theorists fail to understand the prime factors of event-based skills in the exploitation of what they consider player negative expectation games, because such aren't allowed under their definition of reality. In order to understand they would have to dump their entire framework of perception about the truth of the universe, and start over.

The simple truth of all is that every slot machine will pay off, and does pay off, as long as their programming allows for payouts. Under law of the State of Nevada, all slots must pay back at least 75 percent. This means that no slot machine in Nevada can pay less. In fact, most pay a lot more. The average among video slots is a payback of around 94 to 98 percent. This makes the video slots some of the best-paying casino games available—even within the understanding of the mathematical models. Some machines may pay less, others a little more, and machines in states other than Nevada may be set differently. For that information you can write to your local State Regulatory Agency, or whatever the legal body is that regulates casinos and casino games where you live. This is public information, and they must show you the stats, if such are being collected. If this information is not being collected in the state or country where you live, then simply take it under advisement that Nevada standards are those used almost everywhere in the world and that, therefore, no matter where you are playing, the machines you find will most likely pay at an average of around 90 to 94 percent outside of Nevada, and between 94 and 98 percent within the State of Nevada. This is still very good for any casino game, particularly machine-based games.

Even though statisticians and mathematicians conclude that no winning strategy is possible for slots, and certainly not so for video slots, I hope that you have by now realized that their thinking is fundamentally flawed. As a result, their contentions about these games and strategies are irrelevant and largely moot. Which brings us to the strategies for video slots. These machines may "hold" between 2 and 10 percent for the house, but that also means that they have to pay out between 90 and 98 percent. And this in turn means that you can, and will be able to, win on these machines and games—*if* you practice discipline and bankroll management, as well as all of the other Keys to Winning and selections skills I have outlined in the earlier chapter. There is no casino game that cannot be beaten for profit. Some are easier to beat, such as blackjack and live poker, but these are highly skilled games and strategies, and they require much from you and your abilities to play them that way. There are easier strategies for these games, and for other games, and for most of these I refer you to my other books, and in particular to my book *Powerful Profits: Winning Strategies for Casino Games.*

The best advice I can give you here is the best trick of all, and the biggest "secret" of successful gambling, even on slots, and that is this: When you hit for money-value pays, take the win and leave. End the session right then and there, pocket the wins, and start with your originally allocated session stake again, either elsewhere or, under the right cir-cumstances, even on the same game, or machine. Session play is required, and the other skills and abilities are also required. But the best advice is to take the win. Once you cash out, the machine and the casino cannot get that money back unless you are willing to hand it back to them. If you understand this principle, and understand what is meant by session strategies, then you will always wind up with wins at the end of your strategy blocks of sessions, because you will have always left the game *with* the money-value win. If you have forgotten what a money-value win is, read again from the beginning. I mentioned the principle of taking the money-value win, and for going after it, at the very begin-ning of this book.

You may now be wondering if that is all there is to any such strategy for video slots. Well, it isn't. Although such a workable strategy requires us to use our skills and abilities across a broad spectrum of situations, and use an arsenal of knowledge much wider than that usually associated with gambling strategies for some of the other games (blackjack for example), there are some basic hints that go hand-in-hand with the Keys to Winning, and the other disciplines and suggestions I have already made. So, here is a list of do's and don'ts, based on the slot-playing strategy I used in my book *Powerful Profits from Slots*. To be a successful slot player, you will need answers to *at least the majority* of the following:

1. *What is enough time at play?* You must be able to re-main at play for as long as possible in order to be able to reach closest to the machine's optimum payout potential.

2. *What is enough money?* This is what is commonly re-ferred to as the bankroll. In order for you to sustain the re-quired play time, and, depending on the designated machine

you have chosen, you must be able to invest a sufficient amount of money to warrant a successful play period.

3. *How much patience is required?* You must not allow yourself to be distracted or frustrated. Playing video slots is not just entertainment; it's also a financial decision. Investment begets profits, or losses, depending on how well the investor chooses the investment product. In the case of video slot machines, your choices in selection and play, combined with all the Keys to Winning as shown earlier in this book, all constitute your " investment analysis" and "profit potential" scenarios. The old adage of "money makes money" applies to video slots as well. You can't win anything without first making the investment. How you manage the investment is up to you. In slot play, patience, resolve, dedication and "smart" application of your investment goals are necessary for relatively steady success.

4. *What signifies time to quit?* No video slot machine will continuously pay out. They will "take" and "give," usually in cycles. Sometimes you'll find a machine that will simply shower you with wins, while at other times you may get one of the better-paying machines but one which is in the take cycle. To know when to quit is to protect your investment.

5. *When is enough enough?* Well, that's a toss-up. It depends on what the value of the money happens to be for you. Generally, I'd say that any win over and above your initial starting investment is profit, and therefore something you should pocket and keep. Most of the time, in video slots, it is the money-value win that will account for your overall profitability.

6. *How often should I play?* That depends on your available time. Generally, I'd say about once a month, in dedicated periods for profitable play. But that depends, to a large extent, on your time, access to a casino, and available capital. If you play more often, that's okay too, but then you should be more acutely aware of your bankroll and bankroll discipline skills. You should also have a very good grasp of session play and the strategies involved in managing such sessions.

7. *How long should I play?* That also depends on many other factors, particularly your available bankroll and game selection. You should monitor your play and adapt your playing time according to the relevant requirements listed earlier.

8. *Which casino should I play in?* Whichever casinos are in your immediate area, call them first, ask for Public Relations, and have them describe to you the kinds of video slots they have and how many they have. Usually, the more video slots a casino has, the better the overall choices. However, some smaller, or start-up, casinos may also be a good bet for your video slot play, because they may have better-paying machines in order to attract customers. An excellent method for reviewing casinos is to take a really close look at the advertisements they place in gaming magazines, periodicals, and newspapers, or what they provide through direct mail to slot club members. The kind of information you'll want appears in many of these advertisements, periodicals, or flyers, so take advantage of this free information; look, read, and understand. Then call, if you want to know more before you go there. If you can't get any decent information from the PR department, try the Marketing department, or the Player's Club, or even ask for a slot host or casino host.

9. *Which kind of slot machine should I choose?* That has a lot to do with the Keys to Winning (see above). As a rule of thumb, on video slots many of the various bonus pays are actually part of the game's beneficial pay program. All of the advice shown here applies, but the video slots are more complicated and will require more of your dedicated time to learn what the most important play and pay features are.

If you play in this manner you will have a better shot at profitable play more consistently. Of course, you might be one of those very lucky players who will always win, in which case bless you. For the rest of us, I'd stick to the above—and, yes, a little bit of luck every now and then goes a long way for profitable play on video slots.

Probably the biggest benefit of the video slot revolution is the fact that these new video slots offer choices in how much you can bet. Some machines allow for play from 1 coin up to 45 coins per bet, and some of these newest machines up to 500 coins (credits) per spin. This means that the payoffs are also increased proportionately, allowing you to achieve higher wins per hit than was possible on the "older" style machines.

Another beneficial aspect of the newest video slots is the ability to choose the game speed. Some players prefer a slower pace to their game, while many others prefer the game to play fast. I know I do. I find it infuriating if the games play slowly and I don't have the option to change the speed. On many of the newer video slots there's a screen icon that the player can touch to select the speed of the game. I think this is a terrific innovation, because it allows the players to select how *they* wish to play, instead of some programmer deciding the speed for you.

These are just some of the innovations that make video slots among the better games. Here, then, are a few more strategy hints.

10. *How should the machine pay?* Look for machines that pay left to right *and* right to left. Many of the video slots only pay left to right, but machines that allow pays to happen from both directions are often better. There are, however, very few of these games available, and some of the benefits that this initially allowed have been more than compensated for by the greater hit frequency of the machines and games, the better and bigger bonuses, more frequently occurring bonuses, and the introduction of various tiered bonuses and scatter pays. If your choice of games doesn't happen to have pays from both ends, but has the majority of these other features, then it's a good candidate for your investment and play. By this time you have developed enough of a sense of these games that you can make your own informed choices about these two differences in this recommendation.

11. *Which machines pay in multiple combinations?* Look for machines that pay the winning combinations *cumulatively*. Normally, many machines will pay "only the highest winner," which means that if you get more than one winning combination you'll only be paid for the highest win. Since video slots are mostly multi-line machines, meaning there is more than one active payline, it is better for you to play machines that will add up all the wins together, regardless of on which payline they were hit, including multiple wins on the same payline or in the same event.

12. *How many playlines should I look for?* Look for machines that have nine or more paylines, and also include the features from #1 and #2 on page 193. The more paylines you can play, the better the odds for you.

13. *How many coins should I play each pull?* Play maximum coins at all times. Many of these video slots allow you to bet up to 45 coins per bet, and often more, sometimes up to and over 500 coins (credits). This may be a lot of money, but the pays are worth it when you hit any kind of winning combination. If you can't afford this many coins per bet, then play at least the minimum 1 coin requirement per each payline available (9 coins per bet for a 9-line machine, for example). I would recommend, however, that you try to play higher than that. A good median bet is 25 coins per bet (prorated for the number of available paylines on the particular machine at which you happen to be). Nevertheless, you should always remember that if you don't play maximum coins, you will never get the optimum pays and payback of which that machine is capable. The newest video slots are "stepper" payback program machines, just like many video poker games. If you don't play the maximum coins, your payback isn't the most it can be (see my book *Powerful Profits from Video Poker* for how this works, and more details).

14. *Which denomination should I play?* Play the higher-denomination video slots rather than pennies or nickels. The penny and nickel machines may sometimes cost you more to play than you can win (other than perhaps the top award or in case of a giant jackpot progressive). You will gain a better reward from 10-cent and quarter machines than the pennies or nickels on just about every kind of video slot machine (with the exception of some of the newest video slots, such as those shown in earlier chapters of this book).

15. *Which machines should I look for?* Look for machines which have multiple pay symbols that substitute for the majority of other symbols and also have scatter pays; these pay cumulatively. This will give you the best playing options, along with the kinds of features and playing principles described above.

These few additional hints will make your video slot play more enjoyable and also more profitable and can be applied to the vast majority of the new machines you will find in your favorite casino. But—what if you don't win? What if you think you did everything correctly, but you still didn't win? Your visit to the casino, and the sessions you played, didn't produce the wins you thought they should. What then? Was something wrong with you? With your strategy?

Well, there are many factors that could have contributed to this. Here is a short article that I first published in the *Midwest Gaming and Travel* magazine in 2003. It is an important part of any strategy, particularly for video slots.

WHAT IF YOU DON'T WIN?

That great philosopher of the baseball diamond, Yogi Berra, once said: "Winning isn't everything—it's the *only* thing!" Or perhaps it wasn't Yogi who said this—since I can't remember who it was that said it—but I'd like to think that this was yet another "yogi-ism" that makes for such fun in life. Whatever the origin of this may be, it is both correct and wrong at the same time. When we apply this to life, perhaps it is more so than if we apply it to other things, such as video slots. Well, what about video slots? What if you *don't* win?

Sometimes people expect too much, and at other times they expect too little. There are distinct personalities among video slot players that fall neatly into these two categories. The first group are players who *always* expect to win each and every time they play and on each and every spin of the reels, or pull of the handle (or push of the button on the modern machines that no longer have a handle). These are the perennial optimists, so much so that they can almost be called "paranoid optimists" because they are so determined to win that sometimes they overdo it to extremes, and get very depressed if they don't succeed. The other group are the perennial pessimists. These are people who almost *never* expect to win. They are the majority of players who go to casinos to have a good time, play a few coins in the machines, and then move on without even having much of any kind of an expectation of winning. They are the other extreme of the video slot player profile, and the casinos make most of their money from them.

The first group, the perennial optimists, try and try and try again, knowing that they will win something eventually. Although many of these players will likely lose a lot of money before they win, nevertheless they are among the more frequent winners. The other group, the perennial pessimists, don't play nearly as often, or as much in any one sitting, but there are many more millions of them and they rarely win on anything that could be considered a regular basis. These are mostly the kinds of players that writers like myself often describe as the "casual players" or the "tourist players," and so on. In most casino centers, the first group are usually the locals, and the second the friends, relatives, and tourists—the visitors that come only once in a while but don't actually live nearby or work in the industry.

Most locals, and those that work in the casino industry, see almost on a daily basis how often video slots pay out, and how much. There are jackpots in the thousands happening every day, every hour, and often every few minutes in every casino, everywhere. Those local players, and especially those who also work in the gaming industry, see this happening so many times and so frequently that their own gaming becomes tainted by such expectations. This is because the human psyche tends to compartmentalize events and selectively file groups of events into memory by classified category. In this case, the visible frequency of occurrence of such observed wins is classified by the human mind in the category of positive reinforcement derived from the human basic desire to win, in a self-propagating loop that results in a singularized perspective of the frequency of possible recurring wins. What this means is that the human individual invests in his or her own mind singularly occurring events in a group perspective. This is often called the "group identification theory," and in the human psyche as this relates to slot win expectations, it is the group compartmentalization of observed events related to the singular person's own expectations.

Put more simply, the people most frequently exposed to observations of recurring winning events on video slot machines "forget" that these are "different" events on "many" machines over "different" times and under "different" circumstances. Instead, the individual's mind "groups" all these together as a series of "winning events." This, then, leads the individual to perceive winning as something that will "happen frequently."

Mathematically, it is an inevitable hard fact that no gaming machine or gambling game that is inherently a negative expectation game (as most casino games are) will produce regular and recurring wins for the *players*— it will *only* make regular and recurring wins for the *owners*. A video slot machine that holds 2 percent for the house means that it will always hold $2 out of every $100 played through it over the fiscal year life cycle of the machine or game. While this doesn't mean that such a machine will keep $2 out of each $100 you play in it, this *does* mean that when the machine's accounting program is reviewed at the end of each year, its "take" will be at 2 percent, or as near to this as is statistically allowable under the regulatory approval rules that permit minor statistical variations in fractional differentials. This simply means that expecting to win always and all the time is a human psychological condition, often brought about by the brain's inability to completely categorize all human experiences in all of their details, and time-fractional deviations.

Most people easily remember their wins, but not their losses. As with all of the above, this is, again, human nature. We all know that the "good" is remembered more easily than the "bad." We also know that "sensational" news is more interesting than "bland" news. A car seen blowing up on the freeway during the six o'clock news is far more interesting than a report on a pie baking contest at the county fair. While the pie baking contest carries a far greater intrinsic human value, and is a far more positive news item, we tune our TV to the station showing the car blowing up and won't watch the nice lady winning the blueberry pie ribbon. You see, we as humans have a problem with *being* human. While our second group of video slot players never *expect* to win, they would *like* to. These are the people most likely to watch the car blowing up rather than the pie baking contest. This is because they are "passive participants in life's events," watchers and followers rather than actors and initiators. They have a passive interest in video slots and an even more passive interest in winning. When it happens, they usually scream and holler like a banshee, and that's precisely the same kind of adrenaline-infused excitement that they will feel from watching the news report of that car blowing up. This is because in their lives such a rush of adrenaline rarely happens. Mostly this is because they live their lives passively and simply enjoy everything in measured amounts, steadily, with nothing very much out of line with anything else, and never in extremes. These are the people who have steady jobs, and good credit reports, and are always on time to everything, neatly dressed (regardless of what "neatly" may mean in different styles).

So, what if you don't win? Which of the two groups are you in? Where is it you should be? Well, if you are going to be a successful player—video slots or any gambling game—you should be somewhere in the middle. Expect to win, but be mindful of the fact that you may be misperceiving the reality of expectations relative to the exposure to the game, time at game, availability of bank-roll, skills involved, and so on. Winning happens, and regular winnings also happen. However, whether you will be around when they do happen depends on you. Will you be angry when you "do everything right" but don't win? Why? Is it because you played badly, made wrong decisions, and got carried away? If so, whose fault is it? Is it the fault of the method you used, or the strategy you read about? Or is the fault with you? Think about it next time you are going home from the casino after you lost. Was it because you expected to lose and simply allocated that money to your "entertainment"? Or, was it because you expected to win but played badly? Or was it because you got angry and played too much, too long, and for more money than you wanted? Or, did you actually win, but played it all back—and then some?

You see, there are many reasons why people win, and don't win. Most of the people who play video slots actually do win—even a machine that holds 2 percent for the house has to pay out 98 percent. So, if you are lucky enough and catch the machine at the right time, with the right approach, and the right playing strategy, and you win, but then find yourself going home without it, well—what happened? What happened is that you are *human*. You let the event of winning reinforce your brain chemistry and let that make you think that you can do it again, and again, and for more. And so you go home without the win, or with less than you should have. Don't worry, it happens to everybody.

When you don't win, instead of getting angry at the machine, or game, or the person next to you, the cocktail server, casino dealer, your spouse, friends, whomever or whatever, first take a deep breath, sit down and analyze exactly what happened in light of the truth and your own expectations. You may be surprised to find out that what really happened was that you actually won something but didn't keep it. Whatever the decision you made that "cost" you such a win, make yourself remember it. Force your brain to stop categorizing things into groups, and make yourself recognize each *individual* event and occurrence. That way you will be better able to understand yourself, as well as your slot play. And that, dear friends, is how you can make yourself win more often.

Video Slots Payback Percentages

In this chapter I will be able to show you—for the first time anywhere—the actual payback percentages of many of the video slots shown in this book. This is something that you won't usually see in books about video slots, or any slots for that matter. I have the privilege of having access to the *actual data* from the *actual* Par Sheets, the documents used by the very testing laboratories that approve these games for use in the casinos. This information is not readily available, and I want to thank IGT for letting me share it with my readers. Most people don't understand that video slots are among the very best casino games now available. While most people know that games like blackjack, for example, can be played in a skill-based manner that substantially lowers the house hold on that game—and often eliminates it entirely— it is as yet not commonly known that most of the newest video slots have payback programs that include some of the lowest house-hold percentages among all the casinos games. Many of these newest video slots are actually games that hold less than 2 percent for the house, making them quite substantially better—mathematically speaking—than many of the traditionally touted "good" casino games, like craps, blackjack, and baccarat. Some of these video slots have paybacks that are even better than many of the video poker machines, and the reel slots, and that's news!

When you go to the casino, and you find IGT machines and games, and you read the information I have shared with you in this book, you can play comfortably knowing that you are playing simply the best there is. You no longer have to wonder what these machines "hold" and what they "pay back." Now you know, because it's right here, in black and white, plain as day. I don't have room in this book to show you all of the games, and so I have selected some of the most popular video slots, and especially those that I like to play, as examples. They are a window into just how good these games really are. Most of the other IGT games that you are likely to find in your favorite casino will also be within the ranges of these payback percentages, even if it is not one of the games whose actual payback percentage I have listed here. It is enough, in my opinion, to show you a strong cross-section of the kinds of games I have chosen. That should be enough of a guideline for you to find, and play, the best of the video slots.

Here, then, is my selection of some of the video slots I like, along with their paybacks and percentages. When reading this information, you should know what it all means, so I will first explain the headings and the meaning of the information that follows.

Heading	What It Means
Coin	This is the number of coins, or credits, upon which the payback percentage is based. In all my examples, I always use the *maximum coins* for this data. You

Heading	What It Means
	should know, however, that many of the games have lower payback percentages if you don't play maximum coins, or don't play all the lines. There are many such details that I am not showing here because that would take up a whole book by itself. Suffice it to say that if you don't play maximum coins and all the available paylines, you are more than likely not playing the game as well as you can, and as well as you should. So, listen to my *number one* advice one more time: *Always play maximum coins and always play all available paylines.*
Payback	That's the percentage figure that shows the machine's actual payback percentage. It means that the machine will pay back, on average, that many percent of all money played in it. The higher this figure is, the better for you (mathematically speaking).
Hit frequency	This is a number that shows how often the machine and game will hit something. The higher the number, the more frequently the game will have some kind of a paying hit. However, games with a high-hit frequency are not necessarily the best games to play. You should remember some of the other advice you have learned in the previous chapters.
Total hits	This large number shows just how many hits the machine had in its test run. Most

Heading	What It Means
	of the time, machines of this kind are run through their paces at least 10 million times.
Total pays	This equally large number shows just how many pays the machine hit during all those hits. The higher that number, the more pays the machine had.
Max	This is short for maximum coins and means that I have based all this information solely and only on the wager of maximum coins (or credits), whatever that "maximum" may be for that machine or game. To find out what the max coins is for these machines, look it up again in earlier chapters.
Hold	This is the percentage of the house withholding, more commonly know as the house edge. The smaller this number, the better the game. However, sometimes the game may have a higher house hold, but greater hit frequency and for more money-value hits. You see, it is important to know—and note—*all* of this information, and not just some parts of it. This is a mistake that many people make in evaluating casino games, by focusing too much on one statistic, and not taking into account the *totality* of the game in light of the desired objectives—which should be, for most of us, to gain money-value wins (money profits!).

Catch A Wave® Video Slot Machine Pay Table

Coin	Payback	Hit Frequency	Total Hits	Total Pays
Max	98.031%	14.797%	115,057,728	762,291,811
Hold	1.969%			

Cleopatra®™ Video Slots Pay Table

Coin	Payback	Hit Frequency	Total Hits	Total Pays
Max	98.021%	11.549%	3,835,371	23,827,332
Hold	1.979%			

Cops and Donuts™ Video Slots Pay Table

Coin	Payback	Hit Frequency	Total Hits	Total Pays
Max	98.008%	8.968%	26,914,401	294,147,035
Hold	1.992%			

Deep Pockets™ Video Slots Pay Table

Coin	Payback	Hit Frequency	Total Hits	Total Pays
Max	95.506%	7.729%	26,086,104	322,333,599
Hold	2.581%			

Double Diamond® *Fast Hit* Progressive Video Slots Pay Table

Coin	Payback	Hit Frequency	Total Hits	Total Pays
Max	95.580%	10.180%	66,515,460	621,254,190
Hold	1.469%			

The top award and top award return percentage are only available on the 27th coin.

Enchanted Unicorn® Video Slots Pay Table

Coin	Payback	Hit Frequency	Total Hits	Total Pays
Max	98.013%	7.904%	97,868,128	1,028,806,017
Hold	1.987%			

I Dream of Jeannie™ Video Slots Pay Table

Coin	Payback	Hit Frequency	Total Hits	Total Pays
Max	98.060%	8.676%	4,556,895	51,502,967
Hold	1.94%			

Kenny Rogers® The Gambler® Video Slots Pay Table

Coin	Payback	Hit Frequency	Total Hits	Total Pays
Max	98.030%	11.648%	8,077,275	67,978,204
Hold	1.97%			

Lucky Larry's Lobstermania™ Video Slots Pay Table

Coin	Payback	Hit Frequency	Total Hits	Total Pays
Max	97.993%	5.146%	13,351,464	254,233,916
Hold	2.007%			

Money Storm® Video Slots Pay Table

Coin	Payback	Hit Frequency	Total Hits	Total Pays
Max	98.013%	16.979%	8,587,153	35,833,790
Hold	1.987%			

The Munsters™ Video Slots Pay Table

Coin	Payback	Hit Frequency	Total Hits	Total Pays
Max	97.931%	n/a	477,394,158	4,517,756,894
Hold	1.958%			

Phone Tag™ Video Slots Pay Table

Coin	Payback	Hit Frequency	Total Hits	Total Pays
Max	98.043%	5.889%	24,628,188	409,990,246
Hold	1.957%			

Risqué Business™ Video Slots Pay Table

Coin	Payback	Hit Frequency	Total Hits	Total Pays
Max	98.029%	5.349%	27,536,556	504,654,865
Hold	1.971%			

SPAM™ Video Slots Pay Table

Coin	Payback	Hit Frequency	Total Hits	Total Pays
Max	94.987%	8.772%	46,558,263	504,132,940
Hold	5.013%			

Super Cherry®™ Video Slots Pay Table

Coin	Payback	Hit Frequency	Total Hits	Total Pays
Max	98.050%	9.768%	7,332,048	73,601,065
Hold	1.95%			

Tabasco® Video Slots Pay Table

Coin	Payback	Hit Frequency	Total Hits	Total Pays
Max	94.969%	4.216%	15,944,553	363,267,578
Hold	5.031%			

Texas Tea®™ Video Slots Pay Table

Coin	Payback	Hit Frequency	Total Hits	Total Pays
Max	98.010%	10.849%	45,368,803	409,875,440
Hold	1.99%			

The Frog Prince® Video Slots Pay Table

Coin	Payback	Hit Frequency	Total Hits	Total Pays
Max	97.925%	11.648%	8,077,275	63,220,181
Hold	2.075%			

Uncle Sam® Video Slots Pay Table

Coin	Payback	Hit Frequency	Total Hits	Total Pays
Max	97.429%	4.429%	305,966,250	6,731,249,164
Hold	2.571%			

Wild Bear Salmon Run™ Video Slots Pay Table

Coin	Payback	Hit Frequency	Total Hits	Total Pays
Max	98.012%	12.062%	15,763,752	96,217,008
Hold	1.988%			

So, here you have it—a sampling of 20 of the best video slots now available in any casino anywhere, all profiled for you in their naked glory. As you should be able to see, most of these games have very low house-hold percentages, making them truly among the best casino games you are ever likely to find. Therefore, whenever someone says to you something like: "What? Playing video slots? Are you crazy?"—or "Slots are a loser's game" —or "Aren't slots the worst game in the casino?"—well, now you will be able to whip out this book, point to these games, smile, and answer with pride: "Glad you asked, it's about time you were educated in the truth of the real world of the real casinos of the twenty-first century. Hush up, listen, and learn!" Now we can silence all those self-styled casino critics who claim that slots, and video slots, are lousy games. We have the proof. And with such uplifting thoughts, here we are at the end of the book, and that can only mean one thing—time for the Video Slots Quiz!

The Video Slots Quiz

Now comes my favorite part of writing the whole book: The Quiz. I have been a big fan of quiz shows for a long time, two of which are my all-time favorites—*Wheel of Fortune* and *Jeopardy!* Little wonder they also happen to be among my all-time top video slots, right? Well, actually they are included in my list of Top 10 video slots because they happen to be great games. The fact that I personally also like the TV shows didn't influence their selection as part of these lists of video slots. Now, however, I get to have a little fun with my readers, because we can enjoy a sort of quiz show together. If you have also read my earlier Slots book, you are familiar with this Quiz Show concept. For those of you who have not yet read it, here's a little information about how this quiz works.

What follows is a list of questions and several answers. Each question is one to which a successful video slot player should know the answer. Circle the letter you believe is the correct answer. Score 5 points for each correct answer and deduct 5 points for each incorrect answer. (Answers directly follow quiz.) At the end of this chapter you should know how good your video slot player's knowledge really is. All of these questions have a *direct impact* on how well you will do when playing video slots. A high score can significantly improve your chances at consistent wins. So, take out your number 2 pencil and get ready—the time for the test is now.

1. The best kind of video slot machine is
   a. One that looks very interesting.
   b. One that offers multiplier symbols.
   c. One that has really pretty symbols on it.
   d. One that offers multiplier pay symbols that also substitute for most of the others.

2. The best "bonus" video slot machine is
   a. One that has symbols that are wild, or has multiplier symbols which substitute for all other symbols, and also pay scatters.
   b. One that has triple pay symbols or 5 times pay symbols or 10 times pay symbols.
   c. One that has multi-pay symbols that are wild and substitute for all other symbols and pay scatters.
   d. One that has all of the above.

3. It is better to play machines that
   a. Are advertised as "up to 98 percent payback."
   b. Are advertised as "94.7 percent payback."
   c. Are not advertised or promoted at all.
   d. Look like they pay a lot.

4. A "stepper" video slot machine is
   a. One that takes five coins to play.
   b. One that takes nine coins to play.
   c. One that pays more the greater you wager.
   d. One that costs a lot of credits to play.

5. When playing a video slot machine, it is better to play one that
   a. Has five reels.
   b. Has five reels and at least nine paylines or more.
   c. Has three reels.
   d. Has lots of paylines.

6. It is best to play a video slot machine that is
   a. A 25-cent per credit machine.
   b. A 1-penny per credit machine.
   c. A 5-cent per credit machine.
   d. The highest denomination options, the better it is.

7. When playing any video slot machine, it is better to
   a. Sometimes bet one coin and sometimes bet maximum coins.
   b. Often bet less than maximum coins.
   c. Always play maximum coins.
   d. Bet different amounts per spin and vary the betting.

8. The reels on video slot machines are controlled
   a. Mechanically by the use of "stoppers."
   b. By the use of "lead weights."
   c. By computer chips.
   d. By the "luck of the draw."

9. The winning or losing combinations are determined

    a. By luck.
    b. Randomly whenever the reels stop.
    c. As soon as the first coin, or credit, is played.
    d. By the symbols on the reels.

10. All modern video slot machines are
    a. Controlled by a computer and a computer chip.
    b. Controlled by what is known as a random number generator (RNG).
    c. Controlled by changing the payoff program.
    d. All of the above.

11. Video slots are
    a. Better than reel slots.
    b. Worse than reel slots.
    c. Too complicated.
    d. Too hard to hit because of all the combinations and paylines.

12. When playing 45 nickels at a time on a video slot machine, it is better to
    a. Keep at it until you win big.
    b. Better to play this many nickels than less.
    c. Give up because it costs too much.
    d. Go play a 25-cent reel slot machine instead.

13. Playing "penny" video slot machines is
    a. Better than other kinds because it doesn't cost as much to play.
    b. Better because you can last longer and lose less.
    c. Better to not play "penny" machines at all.
    d. Neither better nor worse because it depends on the game and the max bet requirement, which can often be 500 coins per bet, making this a $5 game in reality, or a $3 game at 300 credits, or a $4 game at 400 credits, and so on.

14. The best *average* bankroll for 5-cent video slots is
    a. $50.
    b. $200.
    c. $350.
    d. It depends on the game and how much it requires for optimum play.

15. The best bankroll for any video slot machine is
    a. It depends on your goals and objectives and what you want to gain from the play.
    b. $400.
    c. $600.
    d. $1,000 or more.

16. *Reel* slot machines are
    a. *Better* than video slot machines because they pay better.
    b. *Better* than video slot machines because they are simpler to play.
    c. *Better* than video slot machines because there aren't as many combinations to worry about.
    d. No better or worse than video slot machines because they are in reality both computers.

17. When any slot machine is listed as paying back 98 percent, that means
    a. The machine may pay this much when you play it.
    b. It will pay out this much over the fiscal year life cycle.
    c. It will pay out 98 cents for every dollar you play.
    d. It will pay out that much on average each 50,000 spins.

18. A "jackpot" is
    a. The top amount you can win.
    b. Anything that requires a hand-pay from the atten-
    dant.
    c. Anything that is more than you invested.
    d. Any of the top three amounts listed on the payoff
    display.

19. A "progressive" video slot machine is
    a. Better to play than non-progressives because you
    can win so much more.
    b. Better to play than non-progressives because
    there are more pays.
    c. Not as good as other kinds of slot machines
    which take that many coins.
    d. Worth only a "trial" investment because the odds
    of winning the jackpot are too high.

20. When playing a progressive video slot machine, you
    should
    a. Only bet maximum coins when you feel like it
    will hit.
    b. Sometimes play less than maximum coins to save
    your bankroll and play longer.
    c. Always play maximum coins no matter what.
    d. First see how other people play and then adapt
    what they do.

21. It is better to play a video slot machine
    a. That has 25 coins as maximum bet.
    b. That has 45 coins as maximum bet.
    c. That has 90 coins as maximum bet.
    d. Depending on your bankroll and objectives, but
    all of the above are okay as long as you always
    play maximum coins per spin.

22. Video slot machines are
  a. Better to play because of the multiple lines and betting amounts you can play.
  b. Not as good as regular slots because they are only video screens.
  c. Worse than any other kind of slots because you can't tell what wins.
  d. Worse than any other kind of slots because they cost so much to play.

23. If you're playing a video slot machine that has up to 20 paylines, you should
  a. Only play 1 line.
  b. Only play 3 to 9 lines.
  c. Only play 5 to 10 lines.
  d. Always play all lines.

24. If you're playing a video slot machine that has up to 20 paylines and allows you to bet from 1 coin per line (20-coin bet) up to 5 coins per line (100-coin bet) you should
  a. Never bet the full amount of 100 coins per bet because it's so expensive.
  b. Sometimes bet the full 100 coins and see how the machine is playing.
  c. Bet no more than 25 coins per bet.
  d. Always bet the maximum coins no matter what the total coin-per-bet amount is.

25. The best video slot machines to play, relative to cost of investment, are
  a. Reel video slot machines with 5 reels and 9 lines.
  b. Video slot machines with 5 reels and 20 lines.
  c. Video poker.
  d. Video keno.

Well, that's the end of the questions. Here are the answers, and reasons for them:

Question 1

The answer is *D*. Machines that offer multiplier symbols that double or triple, or pay several times the bet, and also substitute for either all or the majority of the other symbols, are among the very best of all video slots. Most video slots have these symbols, but not all video slots have such symbols that perform all of these functions. Sometimes the multiplier symbols multiply the line bet but do not substitute for the other symbols. This means you first have to hit a winner and then hit it with the multiplier symbol. Other machines have these symbols substituting for some, but not all, of the other symbols. Generally, however, most modern video slots have this favorable combination of such symbols, and that's why the answer to this question is as stated.

Question 2

The answer is *D*. This should be obvious if you got the answer correct for Question 1. Whatever kind of video slot machine it is, if it has multiplier symbols, which are wild *and* substitute for all other symbols *and* pay scatters, then you have a machine that will traditionally pay 98 percent or better as payback. This is the kind you want, but will have to look for and read the payoff display and pay combinations carefully. Even a machine that has at least two of these features will be among the best. One of the best things about video slots is the fact that they all come with pay table screens and help screens. There is a wealth of information there, and if you know how to read this you will be offered a window into the machine's payback program. You won't know exactly, because unlike video poker, video slots aren't defined by the content of the game. If you have looked closely at the chapter on strategies, and seen the payback program sample tables I have shown there, that information in combination with the information about these symbols and how they pay, and how much, will offer you the clearest indication of which video slots are the best.

Question 3

The answer is *B*. Machines that are advertised as "up to . . ." do not *all* have to pay out that amount. If it says "up to," this means that *some* of the machines pay more than that, but *many others pay less*, with the *average* over all the machines so advertised being that percentage. However, machines listed as "payback of 94.7," or any such payback that does *not* have the words "up to" in front of it, means that *all* these machines pay that amount, and not just the average among many of their kind. This applies equally to all slots, reel and video. However, video poker and video keno have their own particular payback programs and payback percentages, and although they are classified as "video slots," they are actually very different. For those paybacks, and other details, I refer you to my books *Powerful Profits from Video Poker* and *Powerful Profits from Keno*.

Question 4

The answer is *C*. A "stepper" slot machine is one whose pays and payback "steps up" as you wager more credits per spin. Unlike "doubler" machines, which merely double the previous pays as you double the bet, stepper slots increase the payback and pays as you wager more. With video slots this means that if you don't play the maximum wager on all available paylines, you will never get either the best payback of which that machine's program is capable, or win the top award at its maximum value. Video poker is a great example of a stepper slot machine: when you bet one coin, two coins, three coins, and four coins, each step of the way the pays are increased proportionately commensurate to the wager. However, on the fifth and final coin wager (for most of the traditional video poker machines) the top jackpot—the royal flush—or even the top several jackpots, such as with Double Double Bonus Poker, the pays are increased much more than would be called for by the simple increment of the extra coin wagered. This next "step" is the reward for playing maximum coins, and the majority of the machine's payback percentage, or at least a very significant portion of it, are vested in that pay. So, if you don't play maximum coins, you will never be able to gain the machine's optimum payback percentage, and you will never be able to gain the machine's jackpot at its maximum value.

Question 5

The answer is *B*. Video slots come in all shapes and sizes, with many paylines and configurations, but almost all come in the 5-reel format. It used to be that 3 reel standard traditional slots were the best, but that was in the days when the 3 reels had only 11 symbols and 11 spaces, for a total of 22 positions. On a 3-reel machine, there would be 22 to the third power—(22^3)—the number of possible combinations, in this case 10,648. That's why most of the old traditional 3-reel slots had only a top jackpot of $10,000, or less. Modern video slots can have as many "stops" and as many "ghosts" (empty spaces) on the virtual reels as the computer programmers wish, allowing for the capacity of the processor. This means that the machines can pay very large jackpots because they are no longer limited by the physical reels that used to be required. The reels that you actually see—regardless of whether they appear as "drums" on a handle puller or as video displays on a monitor—are only the graphic representation of a virtual reel pay table that is nothing more than a bunch of binary numerical strings, equating the number of possible symbols and ghosts and stops on the virtual reels. What you see has absolutely nothing to do with the winning and losing combinations you get.

Video slots that only had 3 reels were tried, and they failed miserably mostly because they were so boring. However, with the advances in computer technology, multiple reels and multiple paylines became possible, as did the various bonusing features that are now part of just about every video slot machine anywhere. For the players, it became better to play machines with multiple reels and multiple paylines, because this meant more pays more often and more chances at the jackpots, and the other significant money-value pays. Soon the 5-reel format became standard, and the 5-line format increased to a 9-line standard. This configuration produces the best possible combination for pays and wins, from the player's perspective. Some of the newest video slots have 20 lines, and even more, but they are all 5-reel video slots. The more lines there are on that 5 reel video slot machine, the better it is for you because you have many more chances to win. That's why you should always play at least the 5-reel and 9-line video slots, and not anything less. The only exceptions to this are the very new *Spin 'n' Hold* video slots I mentioned earlier, because these come in a base 3-reel format.

Question 6

The answer is *D*. The higher the denomination that you can select—depending on your bankroll and financial situation—the better it is for you. The higher denominations pay better, and you will get your money-value wins faster. As you should remember from the early chapters of this book, the money-value wins are those that actually consist of cash wins that are substantially higher than your initial starting bankroll. If you have forgotten the examples I mentioned earlier, go back to the beginning of this book and read those parts again. What most people don't know about video slots is that some of them have different programs that operate on different denominations. This is much more evident in games like video keno, but it can also apply to other video-based games. On such machines, if you play, say, 1 penny per credit, 2 pennies per credit, 5 cents per credit, or 10 cents per credit, the machine will use one program to run the game, and its payback percentage may be lower. This is because it takes many more spins at the lower levels to accumulate the casino's required hold percentage. However, when you select the 25 cent per credit, and higher denominations, the machine switches to a different program, one whose payback percentage may be higher. This is because at these wagers, the casino's hold can be achieved with fewer pulls, and therefore the game can offer a more liberal payback. Although this may not be so for all video slots, there are enough examples of this around that it is important to note. For you, as the player, the most important factor is that the higher the denomination that you play, the shorter will be your exposure to the game, the faster you will get through your session, and the more money-value wins you can accumulate. As with all negative expectation games, the best way to beat them is to hit them fast and go. Approaching these games with one of the playing strategies I have listed in my other book on Slots, and in my book on Winning Strategies, will allow you to maximize your yield from these games by playing them with the highest denomination available. Remember that the longer you play, the more time you are giving the machine's program to average back to its preprogrammed pay and take percentage. So, the answer to beating such games is to play them at the highest possible bet, with the maximum wager on all lines, with a session-based strategy, and hit them and go.

Question 7

The answer is *C*. Never play any video slot machine without the maximum coin bet. If you do, you are giving the casino more profits even if you win; you are not forcing them to pay you the full amount of your win by not playing the maximum coins. You will also never get the best payback that you otherwise could. Don't listen to anyone who says differently, because such proponents don't know a hog from a horse's rear end.

Question 8

The answer is *C.* All modern slot machines—reel and video—are controlled by computer chips, regardless of what they appear to be. There is absolutely no difference between a slot machine with reels that look like they are mechanical and a video reel slot machine. The programs that run them, and the computer chips that control them, are all the same (with different game payout programs for different kinds of machines, but that's not the subject of this question).

Question 9

The answer is *C.* As soon as the first coin or credit(s) trips (clocks) the machine's sensors, the end-result combinations of that spin or pull are already determined. The fact that it takes a few seconds for the reels to stop is just window dressing. The machines have a program that runs millions of possible combinations per micro-second, and the instant the coin or credit trips the sensor, this process stops and decides the outcome of that spin. These combinations become "frozen" for the duration of that spin (event) on the machine's virtual reels, and when the graphic display stops and shows it to you, and your win is paid if you had a win, then the program goes back to the scans of millions of possibilities until the next time you clock the game with your next play. And yes, playing maximum coins is still the best way to play. It allows you to cash in on the payoffs closest to the true odds of the machine's payoff program, especially on the "buy-a-pay" machines (which many of the bonus games are) particularly those that offer tiered second- and third-screen bonuses.

Question 10

The answer is *D*. All modern slot machines are controlled by a computer, which has what is commonly referred to as the RNG, a program that controls the randomness of the combinations. All video slots are controlled by changing the payoff programs to whatever the casino wants them to be, usually by means of changing the game's programming chip (which has to be done in accordance with gaming regulations and must be reported and supervised and verified, so no "cheating" is possible).

Question 11

The answer is *A*. Video slots are much better to play than any other kind of slots because of the tremendous pays that can be achieved by the use of multiple paylines and multiple coins per bet. The fact that you can bet 45 coins—or more—per spin means that you will be getting much better overall payouts than on any other kind of machine, when you hit. It is also a plain fact that many of these video slots can easily be found with paybacks of 98 percent and more, as you can see from the chapter on paybacks where I have listed some of them and showed you how they are configured. This makes video slots among the best casino games to play, and certainly very much in line with the best video poker games, as well as blackjack, craps, and even baccarat.

Question 12

The answer is *B*. Whatever denomination you play, be it nickels, pennies, dimes, quarters, or more, the answer is still the same: It is always better to play the 45 coins per spin on a machine whose maximum wager is this many coins (credits), than to play the game for less. If the machine takes 25 coins per spin, then the 25 coins would be the answer. If the machine takes 90 coins per spin, then that will be the answer. I realize that in many cases this will seem like a lot of money, but if you want to play video slots for powerful profits, you can't play them only for their entertainment value. There are many books and articles that recommend you play 1 coin per line, or only a few coins, and so on. This may be okay if all you play for is entertainment, but it is surefire financial suicide if you want to play to win money. There is simply no other answer and no in-between. Video slot machines have programs and paybacks that are top heavy, and this means that if you don't play the maximum coins you will never get the best the machine can offer and therefore are assured of only two facts: (1) you will be entertained and (2) you will be a loser. Playing video slots for anything less than the maximum wager simply means you are throwing your money out and burning it at a very fast rate. You will never gain anything even close to either the game's optimum payback or the kind of money-value wins that are the key to beating games like these, that are by their program a negative expectation game. You simply can't outlast them, and that's something with which I agree even if it means agreeing (at least temporarily) with the limited mathematical perspective of the games. Your exposure to these games—by the very nature of casino gambling—will be so short, and so finite, that your only means to win consistently is to do what I have already shown, and that is to play a session-based strategy, with the proper bankroll, at the highest denomination possible, and always for maximum wagers, and always hit and take it and go (allowing for the take-home money-value wins, and also allowing for the remaining principles of the session strategy you may be using).

Question 13

The answer is *D*. No matter what the denomination, keep in mind what this means in real money. A "penny" machine that takes 500 coins (credits) per pull is in reality a $5 slot machine. Therefore, the answer to this question directly depends on the game and the circumstances. Although the higher denominations are better, in this case a video slot machine that may be shown as being a penny game, but one that can be played for $5 per pull, may be a lot better than a game that is shown as nickels but that only takes 45 coins ($2.25) per pull. The penny game at $5 per pull may—in this instance—be a better bet. That's why it is oh-so-important for you always to choose your machine and game wisely, and know what it is you are getting before you go and get it.

Question 14

The answer is *D*. Refer also to the chapter on Keys to Winning, and modify your personal bankroll accordingly, if your playing preferences so dictate.

Question 15

The answer is *A*. If you got the answer correct for the previous question, then this should also have been obvious. In gambling, the answer to most questions is: It depends. This is because so much depends on the circumstance, and the situation, both for the game and the player. What kind of a game is it? What is your objective? How much money do you have? What can you reasonably afford? What are your goals? Generally speaking, you should never approach any video slot machine with less than $400, assuming, of course, that you have taken my advice and will always play maximum coins. However, this again depends on the machine, game, you, your situation, and so on. Make your bankroll decision according to the max bet value of the game you wish to play.

Question 16

The answer is *D*. There is no inherent difference between reel slot machines and video slot machines (other than the payback programs, but that isn't the subject of this question). In fact, reel slot machines *are* video slot machines, and their programming principles are the same as any other video slot machine. Just because you see "reels" in the window makes no difference. You could be seeing anything else, and it would still be the same. It's the chip inside that holds the machine's game. The rest is just the box and the display.

Question 17

The answer is *B*. The payoff percentages listed are *averages* over a yearlong cycle based on millions of pulls. Such machines will, in the end, pay out this much, all pays and hand pays combined. It will *never* pay out 98 cents for each coin played, nor will it pay you $98 out of each $100 for that particular session. It may pay more, or less, when you happen to be sitting there playing it, but overall in the end all such pays will equal 98 percent of all the money played through the machine, or as close as is statistically feasible and acceptable. And so on for any machine that is listed as paying back a specified *flat* percentage.

Question 18

The answer is *C*. If you have made a profit, *any* kind of profit, you are way ahead of the reality of the machine's pre-programmed house edge. Therefore, it is a jackpot, even if it is only $1, or even less. Whatever the amount is that you have made *over and above your initial investment* is a jackpot, and means you have defeated the house edge by a huge percentage differential!

Question 19

The answer is both *C*, and/or *D*. Progressives do not pay well because some of the money goes to build the giant progressive top award (the generally accepted estimate is from about 5 percent to 10 percent of all the money put through the machines that are part of such a progressive link). These machines are good to play occasionally, for a "trial" investment, but you are far better off playing other kinds of video slots that take the same number of coins as maximum. (Score +5 points if you picked *either* C or D.)

Question 20

The answer is *C*. If that isn't obvious, you'll need to revisit your school for some extra lessons in arithmetic. Remember this, and remember it well: *You can't win the giant award on any progressive machine if you do not play the maximum coins!* Period!

Question 21

The answer is *D*. Again the same principles apply as those already stated in answers to previous questions. It depends. It depends on a multitude of factors, and each of these will be particular to each player and specific circumstances. Only you can make those final and finessed judgments, because you know yourself and your situation. What I can do is offer you a guideline, and as much information as I can put into this book, and my other books, so that you are empowered with as many opportunities to make the best possible choices as they apply to you and your situation. In this way, the phrase "it depends" will take on specific meaning to you and your specific situation. In this question, the answer speaks for itself, and your situation will determine which of these options will be better suited to you under those given situations and circumstances.

Question 22

The answer is *A*. Video slots are so much better than any other kind of slot machine *precisely because* they allow for so many paylines, pay options, and higher maximum coin limits (understanding that you have now learned to *select* the correct machines and learned what they do and how they pay, and thus are able to apply your skills and knowledge to the betterment of your decisions).

Question 23

The answer is *D*. Always play all lines, and for maximum wagers. Earlier answers should have made this clear, and you should know this by now. If you think you "can't afford" to play at these levels, either don't play, save up and play when you can, or realize that you are not a player who can, or will want to, play to make profits. You may simply be one of those players that likes to pay to be entertained, and if that's so it's perfectly okay to be such a player. However, the answer to this question—as indeed all the others—has to do with players who want to make money at these games, and therefore play them for profit. That makes the situation a lot different from those who simply like to play a little here and a little there, for entertainment.

Question 24

The answer is *D*. See how easy it is when you pay attention? Check out the answer to the above question. Isn't it nice how clear it all becomes once you start understanding the principles of playing for profit, and the difference between playing that way or playing only as a means of paying to be entertained?

Question 25

The answer is *D*. As curious as this may sound to some, video keno offers the best payouts *relative to cost of investment* of any kind of video slot machine. And yes, it is a video slot machine. For a 25-cent bet, you can win over $5,000 on some combinations, and that's a huge payoff potential relative to the base investment. Therefore—and *only* for video keno—I advise that the general "always play maximum coins per bet" be modified. *Only for Video Keno!!* On this game, and *this game only*, you can bet less than maximum coins and still get a very high payoff relative to the amount invested. You see, again it depends—on the game, you, the paybacks, the lines, the kinds of games, and so on and on. Now you know just how different gambling on video slots can be, and how much more to it there is than just the pretty pictures and the simplicity of pushing the buttons.

Scoring

Give yourself 5 points for each correct answer, and take away 5 points for each wrong answer. Score your totals as follows:

100–125 total points   You are a professional! You should form a video slot syndicate and play all the time. This means you are the Guru of Video Slots. Congratulations!!

75–95 total points   You are very good! But you could use a little more study.

50–70 total points   You need some help, but you're pretty good.

25–45 total points   You're obviously playing just for entertainment and aren't particularly concerned with winning. Perhaps you should try something different, like fishing.

Below 25 total points   Casinos *love you!!* They will invite you back over and over again, because they know they'll get all your money all the time. Save yourself the trip and just mail the money in. Or, better still, mail it to me. I'll play it for you, and when I win I'll send you back a 10 percent profit. Better than any stock market, right?

And that's the end of this quiz.

Postscript

In this book you have seen the future of casino gambling. The video slots I have shown you are the cutting edge of the current technological revolution. Many of the games in this book are only now appearing in casinos throughout the United States, and elsewhere in the world. They are the very latest of the video gaming machines that have taken casinos by storm over the past decade. And they are only the beginning. Even as you are reading this paragraph, there are great new innovations already planned. Many are done and ready, waiting only on the players to catch up to the technology. The future of the modern casino will be even more remarkable than the games we now know. Holographic video slots, for example, are already a reality, even though not yet on the casino floor.

There are currently designs being made for what is about to be called the total gaming experience, or TGE for short. These are self-contained and enclosed kiosks that contain a virtual casino. These will be placed on the casino floor, kind of like the big arcade games where you have to get inside and sit down to play the game. In this modern casino version, you would step inside this kiosk, sit in a sumptuously comfortable chair with all the amenities handy, such as drink holders. Surrounding you will be a surround-sound wide screen plasma digital TV display. As you walk in and sit down, the kiosk will come to life and the games will welcome you. You will be greeted, asked to insert your player's card, your credit or bank cards, or your casino credits, and select from a multitude of menus. Later models will include a complete virtual reality, where the entire casino experience will unfold in front of you in holograms. You will activate the games and your choices by touching virtual icons that will appear as holographic images all around you. All the games will play in 3-D, and you will be in the middle of it all. Not just video slots, but any kind of casino game, even new games that require knowledge and skills. Such games are already partially here, and more are coming. The future of casino gaming, and especially video and holographic gaming, is here already, and there are only three reasons why you are not yet seeing these kinds of innovations in your favorite casino.

First, there is the matter of player acceptance. Current casino players aren't ready for these kinds of "futuristic" games and gaming innovations. The adults who now come to the casino grew up barely familiar with the earliest forms of rudimentary video gaming. They know about primitive games like Pong, for example, where you would control two paddles either side of the monitor and play a kind of tennis game. These casino players still like the traditional feel of the games, such as slots with handles to pull. Even though many such players have already embraced video slots (and, as you saw from this book, for good reasons) nevertheless they aren't as ready to go even farther into the wide world of technological innovation. Modern casino innovations in video gaming have to wait for the video arcade generation to make a bigger impact. These players are already here, and that's why we have more of an acceptance of video and computerized gambling. However, these players are from the generation that still prefers game "themes" as opposed to just liking video and computer gaming, based on its appeal and content, and regardless of any familiar "theming." That's why the current crop of video slots are based so much in familiar themes, like old TV shows and game shows. That's to attract the arcade generation by means of familiar themes to which they will respond. The real video and computer gaming innovations have yet to wait for the computer and computer and video game generation to grow up. These are the kids who were born after 1984, and grew up with home computers, computer games, the Internet, Play Station and the X-Box video games. None of these players are as yet 21 years of age, and therefore they can't gamble in many casinos, and those who are old enough to play don't number enough players to make a commercial impact. This will change very soon, and very rapidly. Within the next 5 to 10 years, most of the computer kids will become adults, and as their economic power grows and they start to have disposable incomes, they will flock to casinos where they can play video and computer games for real money, as opposed to only the pride of being the best on the X-Box or Play Station. As they, and their kids grow up, so the casinos of the 2010s, and into 2020s will suddenly become the kind of "futuristic" casinos whose games and technology we now only see on *Star Trek* and its holodecks.

The second reason why you aren't seeing these kinds of futuristic games in the current casinos has to do with the game technology. Although almost all the technology and innovations and ideas already exist, much of the technology is still bulky and not as yet fully executed. This has to wait for faster processors, more memory, better storage units like micro-CDs (my invention, incidentally), and the rest of the fast-growing casino-related computer hardware technology. Most of this will be ready in about two or three years, but even then it will still have to wait for the customers and casino players to catch up to it.

The third reason is government regulation and regulatory approvals. Just as the innovations in casino games have to wait for the public to catch up in acceptance of such new games, so regulators have to catch up to understanding what these new gaming innovations are and how they will work. Gaming regulators are people with skills in computer technology, and they have to learn how to test and approve these innovations. Then, the legislatures of the various gaming jurisdictions have to approve such radically different casino games for use in their casinos. All this takes time because governments move slowly. Eventually, however, it will all come together. The future will bear out the lessons of the past, and we will get there in a hurry, albeit slowly in such humanly measured speed of progress.

And so, dear reader, the future of casino video slots and video and computerized gaming is already all around us. We just aren't seeing it yet. In the words of the great statesman, Winston Churchill: "This is not the end. It is not even the beginning of the end. But it is, perhaps, the end of the beginning."

I wish you the best of success!

Trademarks and Copyrights

Throughout this book, I mentioned several slot machines, which are products, either owned by, or often based upon registered, copyright, and trademark ownership of either IGT or third parties. All are used herein by permission. The following information acknowledges such ownership of these products, images, logos, and other distinctive features as indicated.

IGT® AND THIRD-PARTY TRADEMARK LISTS

The following are registered, copyright, and/or trademark by International Game Technoogy (IGT), of Reno, Nevada, used by permission:

100 for 1™
The $1,000,000 Pyramid™
18 Reeler™
21 Gambler®
4th of July®
7s Wild® (Canada Registration)
8 Ball®
Ace$ Bonus Poker®
Ace in the Hole®
Aces and Faces™
The Addams Family™

The Addams Family™
  Cousin It™
Alien
Arabian Riches®
Austin Powers™
Austin Powers™ *International-Game of Mystery*™
Austin Powers™ *Time Portal*
Austin Powers™
  Goldmember™
Balloon Bars® (Nevada Registration)

Beachcomber Joker Poker™
Beetle Bailey®
Beetle Bailey's® *One-Day
  Pass*
Benny Big Game
The Beverly Hillbillies™
The Beverly Hillbillies™
  Clampett's Cash
The Beverly Hillbillies™
  Bubblin' Crude™
The Beverly Hillbillies™
  Moonshine Money
Big Times Pay®
Big Wheel of Gold®
Bitblitz®
Black Cherry®
Black Jack®
Blackout Poker®
Black Rhino®
Black Tie®
Black Widow®
Bogart and Bergman™
Bonus Poker™ (Nevada
  Registration)
Bonus Wheel™
Boulder Dash™
Bull Market™
Bulls-Eye®
By George®
Cabby Cash®
Candy Bars®
Cashablanca™
Cash Advance™
Cash Convoy™
Cash Quest®

Casino Night®
Catch a Wave®
Cats 'n' Dogs®
Cats 'n' Dogs® *Spin 'n' Hold*
Caveman Keno®
Chainsaws & Toasters®
Champagne and Caviar™
Chaos®
Checkmate®
Chocolate Bars™
Cigar™
Cleopatra®
Cleopatra™
Colorado Nickels®
Congo Quest®
Cool Millions®
Cops and Donuts™
Coral Reef®
*Creature from the Black
  Lagoon*
Crystal Fives™
Crystal Sevens®
CVT-Plus™
The Dating Game
Deep Pockets™
Deuces Joker Wild Poker™
  (Nevada Registration)
Deuces Wild™
Deuces Wild Bonus Poker®
Diamond Cinema™
Diamond Cinema® *Frank
  Sinatra*™ *Gift Wheel*™
Diamond Cinema® *Frank
  Sinatra*™ *Dice*™
Diamond Cinema® *Frank*

Sinatra™ *Sinatra Record*™
Diamond Cinema® James Dean™
Diamond Cinema® Steve McQueen™
Diamond Fives®
Diamond Mine™
Diamond Run™
Diamond Tens™
Dilbert's Wheel Bert
Dimes Deluxe™
Dollars Deluxe®
Double American Beauty®
Double Black Tie™
Double Bonus Poker™
Double Bucks®
Double Desire®
Double Diamond®
Double Diamond 2000®
Double Diamond Deluxe®
Double Diamond® *Fast Hit*™
Double Diamond Mine®
Double Diamond Run™
Double Diamond® *Spin 'n' Hold*
Double Dollars® (Nevada Registration)
Double Dollars™
Double Double Bonus Poker®
Double Double Diamond Luck™
Double Double Dollars®

Double Down Stud®
Double Dribble™ (Nevada Registration)
Double Hearts™
Doublemania™ (Nevada Registration)
Double Pay™
Double Red White & Blue™
Double Strike™
Double Ten Times Pay™
Double Top Dollar®
Double Triple Diamond Deluxe with Cheese™
Double Wild®
Double Your Money™
Dragon's Gold™
Draw 80™ (Montana Registration)
Draw 80 Plus™ (Montana Registration)
Earthquake™ (Nevada Registration)
EDT™ (Nevada, New Jersey Registration)
Elephant King®
Elizabeth Taylor Dazzling Diamonds
Elvira® Mistress of the Dark
Enchanted Unicorn®
Evel Knievel™
EZ Pay™
EZ Play™
EZ Route™
Fabulous 50s®
Famous Games™

Fancy Fruits®
Fast Action Five Play Draw Poker™
Fast Action Ten Play Draw Poker™
Fast Action Triple Play Draw Poker™
Fast Money™
Fiesta Bucks™
Fire & Fortune™
Fishin' Buddies®
Fistful of Dollars™ (Nevada Registration)
Five Card Instant Bingo®
Five Deck Frenzy™
Five Play™
Five Play Draw Poker™
Five Star™
Five Times Pay™
Five Times Pay (Black & White)™
Five Times Pay Red White & Blue™
Fortune Cookie™
Fortune Reel™ (Nevada, New Jersey Registration)
Four Deck Draw®
Four Play Blackjack™
Fourth of July®
Four Times Pay™
Fox 'n' Hound®
Free Fall Poker™
Free Kick®
Frequent Flyer®
The Frog Prince®

Fruit Falls®
Full House®
Game King™
Game King Plus™
Ghost Island
Go Bananas®
Gold Digger™
Gold Fever™ (New Jersey Registration)
Gold Mountain®
Gold Silver & Bronze®
Good Times™
Gopher Cash®
Gravy Train™
The Great Turkey Shoot™
Happy Camper™
Harley-Davidson®
Haywire!®
Hexbreaker
High Rollers™
Hit the Top®
Home Run®
Hot Hand™
Hot Peppers®
Hot Shot™
Hula Hula®
Hula Moolah™
Hundred or Nothing™
Hurricane®
Hurricane is Wild™ (Nevada Registration)
iGame®
I Dream of Jeannie™
iGame (Interactive Game)®
iGame-Plus™

IGT®
IGT.com®
IGT Gaming Systems™
IGT's Guide to Video
  Gaming™
IGT University®
IGT University™
I Love Lucy®
Instant Bingo™
Integrated Voucher
  System™
International Game
  Technology®
It Ain't Over Until the Fat
  Lady Sings™
It's a Blast
IVS™
Jackpot Devil™ (Nevada
  Registration)
Jackpot Jewels®
Jackpot Jungle®
Jackpot Poker™
Jacks or Better™
Jekyll & Hyde™
Jeopardy!®
Jeopardy!® Tournament of
  Champions™
Jeopardy!® Tournament of
  Champions™ Free Spin™
Jester®
Jewel in the Crown™
Joe's Yard Games
Joker (Joker Head)™
Kangaroo®

Kenny Rogers® The
  Gambler®
Keno Deluxe™
Kingpin Bowling
Knockdown®
Laverne & Shirley
Leap Frog®
Leopard Spots®
Lifestyles of the Rich and
  Famous®
Lion Fish®
Little Devil®
Little Green Men®
Little Green Men™
Little Green Men, Jr.™
Little Green Men™ Spin 'n'
  Hold
Livin' Large™
Lock & Roll®
Loose DEUCE DEUCES
  Wild®
Louisiana Louie®
Louisiana Nickels®
Lucky 7's®
Lucky Deal Poker®
Lucky Ducks™
Lucky Larry's
  Lobstermania™
Mag 7®
Magic Wish™
Market Madness™
M*A*S*H™
Masterlink™
Matrix Poker®
Mayan Wheel of Gold®

Megabucks®
MegaJackpots™
MegaJackpots Instant
  Winners™
MegaKeno®
Mega Mystery™
Mega Poker®
Megasport®
Midnight Madness™
Mississippi Megabucks®
Mississippi Nickels®
Money Storm®
Moolah!®
Moonshine Money™
Ms. Little Green Men™
Mucho Dinero™
Multi-Card Keno™
Multi-Denomination®
Multi-Denomination™
Multi-Line Madness™
Monster Mansion
The Munsters™
My Rich Uncle™
Mystery Millions™
Mystical Mermaid
Neon Casino®
Neon Nights®
Neon Poker®
Nevada Nickels®
The Newlywed Game
Nickelmania®
Nickels Deluxe®
Nurse Follies
Olympic Gold™ (Nevada
  Registration)

One Pull Can Change Your
  Life®
On the Prowl®
Party Time®
Patriot Poker™ (Nevada
  Registration)
The Phantom of the
  Opera™
Phone Tag™
Pick to Win®
Play Ball™ (Nevada
  Registration)
Player's Choice Poker™
  (Nevada Registration)
Player's Edge®
Player's Edge-Plus®
Play It Again Poker™
Pokermania®
Polly's Poker®
Powerbucks™
Power Keno®
Price Check®
The Price is Right™
The Price is Right™ Punch
  a Bunch™
The Price is Right™
  Showcase Showdown™
Psycho Cash Beast®
Psycho Fat Lady™
Pure Pleasure®
Quartermania®
Quarters Deluxe®
Quick Cash™
Quick Draw™ (Nevada
  Registration)

Quick Silver™ (Nevada
  Registration)
Quiz Show™
Racing 7's™
Rapid Jackpot®
Razzle Dazzle®
Red Ball®
Red Hot 7's®
Red, White & Blue®
Red, White & Blue™
Regis' Cash Club™
*Richard Petty Driving
  Experience*™
Rich Girl®
Risqué Business™
River Gambler®
*Rodney Dangerfield Reel
  Respect*
Royal Flush®
Royal Riches®
Run for Your Money®
*Run for Your Money
  Deluxe*®
S2000™
S2000-I™
Sale of the Century
Sands of Gold®
Satellite®
Score Board®
Senet®
Set 4 Life®
Sevens Up®
Seven Times Pay™
Shark Hunter™
Shock Wave™

Shocking Headlines
Shooting Gallery®
Shore Money™
Sierra Silver®
Sinatra™
Sizzling 7®
Slam Dunk®
Slingo™
Slot King™
Slot Line®
Slot View®
Slotopoly®
Slotto™ (Nevada, New
  Jersey Registration)
Smart System®
Smashmouth Football™
S'mores®
Spell Binder®
Spiker the Biker™
Spin 'n' Hold
Spin Poker™
Spin Til You Win®
S-Plus™
S-Plus Limited™
Spooky Slots™
Star Wars
Stinkin' Rich™
Strike®
Sugar & Spice®
Sugar Daddy™
Super 8 Race®
Super Cherry®
Super Cherry™
Super Double Pays®

Super Joker™ (Nevada Registration)
Super Mag7®
Super Nickelmania™
Super Spin Sizzling 7™
Super Stars®
Tailgate Party™
Take Your Pick®
Temperature's Rising®
Temple of Gold®
Ten Play Draw Poker™
Ten Times Pay®
Ten Times Pay™
Ten Times Pay Red, White & Blue™
The Terminator™
Texas Tea®
Texas Tea™
Tidal Wave®
Time Warp®
Titanic™
Top Dollar®
Top Dollar Deluxe®
Totally Puzzled
Touchdown™ (Nevada Registration)
Touchscreen™
Treasure Trail™
Triple Bonanza®
Triple Bonus Poker®
Triple Bucks™
Triple Cash™
Triple Cat™
Triple Diamond®
Triple Diamond Deluxe®

Triple Dollars®
Triple Double Diamond®
Triple Double Dollars™
Triple Double Five Times Pay™
Triple Double Red, White & Blue™
Triple Jackpot®
Triple Jackpot 3 x 9®
Triple Lucky 7's®
Triple Lucky 7's™
Triple Play™ (Nevada Regstration)
Triple Play Draw Poker™
Triple Play Five Play Draw Poker™
Triple Play Five Play Ten Play Replay™
Triple Play Replay™
Triple Red, White & Blue™
Triple Sapphires®
Triple Stars®
Triple Texas Tea™
Triple Wild®
Triple Zesty Hot Peppers®
Tropical Fever™
TV Hits™
Twelve Times Pay™
The Twilight Zone®
Uncle Sam®
UNO®
Triple UNO® *Bonus*
UNO® *Attack*® *Scatter Pay*
Used Cars

Victory™ (Nevada Registration)
Video Megabucks®
Vision Series®
Volcano®
Wheel & Deal®
Wheel of Fortune®
Wheel of Gold™
Whirl Win®
White Ice™
White Stars®
Wild Bear®
Wild Bear Salmon Run™

Wild Cherry®
Wild Cherry Pie®
Wild Cherry® *Spin 'n' Hold*
Wild Diamonds®
Wild Dolphins
Wild Five Times Pay™
Wild Star®
Wild Taxi™
Wild Thing!®
Win Place Show™ (Nevada Registration)
Winner's Choice®
Young Frankenstein

THIRD-PARTY TRADEMARK LISTS

The following are registered, copyright, and/or trademarked by International Game Technology (IGT), of Reno, Nevada, and/or by third parties under appropriate arrangements between IGT and such third parties, and are used by permission:

- *$1,000,000 Pyramid*™ © 2002 CPT Holdings, Inc. All rights reserved. Mark requires ™.
- *$1,000,000 Pyramid*™ © 2003 CPT Holdings, Inc. All rights reserved. Mark requires ™.
- *$25,000 Pyramid*™ © 2003 CPT Holdings, Inc. All rights reserved. Mark requires ™.
- *The Addams Family*™ Developed under agreement with Monaco Entertainment Corporation. "Uncle Fester" image ™/© 2002 & 2003. The Estate of Jackie Coogan licensed by Global Icons, Los Angeles, CA 90034. All rights reserved. Mark requires ™.

- *American Bandstand*® © 2003 dick clark productions, inc. All rights reserved. Mark requires ®.
- *Ardac*® Registered trademark ® of Money Controls.
- *Austin Powers*™ © MMIII New Line Productions, Inc. *Austin Powers*™ and all related names, characters, and indicia are trademarks of New Line Productions, Inc. 2003. All rights reserved.
- *Austin Powers*™ New Line Productions, Inc. © 2002 New Line Productions, Inc. All rights reserved. Mark requires ™.
- *Beetle Bailey*™ © 2002 King Features Syndicate Inc. TM The Hearst Corporation. Mark requires ™
- *The Beverly Hillbillies*™ © 2003 CBS Worldwide, Inc. All rights reserved. Mark requires ™.
- *Bewitched*™ © 2003 CPT Holdings, Inc. All rights reserved. Mark requires ™.
- *Bloopers*™ *Bloopers* © 2001 is a trademark of dick clark productions, inc. All rights reserved. Mark requires ™.
- *Cash King Checkers*™ Trademark of IGT. Developed under agreement with Leading Edge Design, LLC. Mark requires ™.
- *The Chicken Game*™ Developed under agreement with Plan Bee Productions.
- *Creature from the Black Lagoon*™ Trademark and copyright of Universal Studios. Licensed by Universal Studios Licensing LLLP. All rights reserved. Mark requires ™.
- *Dick Clark's Censored Bloopers*™ © 2003, a trademark of dick clark productions, inc. All rights reserved.
- *Dick Clark's New Year's Rockin' Eve*® Logo requires ®.
- *Elvira*® *Elvira* and *Mistress of the Dark* are trademarks of Queen "B" Productions. Rights used by permission. *Elvira's Haunted Hills* is the copyright and

trademark of Elvira Movie Company, LLC. Rights used by permission. *Elvira* mark requires ®, Mistress of the Dark mark requires ™.

- *Elvis*®   *Elvis, Elvis Presley,* and *King of Rock 'n' Roll* are registered trademarks of Elvis Presley Enterprises, Inc. © Elvis Presley Enterprises, Inc. Mark requires ®.
- *Evel Knievel*™   © 2003 Robert Craig Knievel aka Evel Knievel. Mark requires ™.
- *EZ Pay*™   Trademark of IGT.
- *Family Feud*™   *Family Feud* and related marks are trademarks of FremantleMedia Operations B.V. Based on the FremantleMedia television program *Family Feud.* Licensed by Fremantle Brand Licensing (www.fremantlemedia.com). Mark requires ™.
- *Fifty Play Draw Poker*™   Action Gaming multi-hand poker games utilize U.S. Patents 5,823,873; 6,007,066; 6,098,985; and other patents pending that are licensed from Action Gaming, Inc., and must be operated under separate license agreements with IGT. Mark requires ™.
- *Harley-Davidson*™   © 2003 H-D. All rights reserved. Mark requires ®.
- *Honeymooners*™   Used under license. Mark requires ™.
- *Humphrey Bogart*™   © 2001 Bogart, Inc. Licensed by CMG Worldwide (www.cmgww.com). Mark requires ™.
- *I Dream of Jeannie*™   © 2002, 2003 CPT Holdings, Inc. All rights reserved. Mark requires ™.
- *I Love Lucy*®   Registered trademark of CBS Worldwide, Inc. Images of Lucille Ball and Desi Arnaz are licensed by Desilu, too, LLC. Licensing by Unforgettable Licensing. Mark requires ®.
- *Indigo Swing*™   Developed under agreement with Signature Games. Mark requires ™.

- *Ingrid Bergman*™ © 2001 Estate of Ingrid Bergman licensed by CMG Worldwide (www.cmgww.com). Mark requires ™.
- *JCM*® JCM and the JCM logo are registered trademarks of Japan Cash Machine Co. Ltd. and JCM American Corporation.
- *Jeopardy!*® Registered trademark of Jeopardy Productions, Inc. *Jeopardy!* © 2003 Jeopardy Productions, Inc. All rights reserved. Mark requires ®.
- *Let's Make a Deal*® Trademark of *Let's Make a Deal*. Registered in the United States and pending elsewhere, and is used under license. Mark requires ®.
- *Lifestyles of the Rich and Famous*® © 2003 Rysher Entertainment, Inc. All rights reserved. Mark requires ®.
- *Marilyn Monroe*™ © Marilyn Monroe, LLC, licensed by CMG Worldwide (www.cmgww/MarilynMonroe.com). Mark requires ™.
- *MEI ZT 1200*® Registered trademark of Mars, Incorporated.
- *The Mummy*™ Trademark and copyright of Universal Studios. Licensed by Universal Studios Licensing LLLP. All rights reserved. Mark requires ™.
- *The Munsters*™ Copyright of Kayro-Vue Productions and a trademark of Universal Studios. Licensed by Universal Studios Licensing LLLP. All Rights Reserved. Developed under agreement with Monaco Entertainment Corporation. Designed under agreement with Game Refuge, Inc. and Great Circle Gaming Corporation. Mark requires ™.
- *Othello*® © 2003 J.A.R. Games Co. All rights reserved. Licensed by J.A.R. Games Co. Mark requires ®.
- *Richard Petty Driving Experience*™ Mark requires ™.

- *The Pink Panther*™   *The Pink Panther* and associated trademarks and characters ™ & © 2003 United Artists Corporation. All rights reserved. Mark requires ™.
- *The Price Is Right*™   Trademark of FremantleMedia Operations B.V. Based on the FremantleMedia TV Program *The Price Is Right.* Licensed by Fremantle Brand Licensing (www.fremantlemedia.com). Mark requires ™.
- *Sinatra*™   An IGT product manufactured in association with Sheffield Enterprises, Inc. and Bristol Productions Limited Partnership. Mark requires ™.
- *South Park*™   © 2003 Comedy Central. All rights reserved. Comedy Central mark requires ®, *South Park* mark requires ™.
- *SPAM*™   *SPAM* and related marks are trademarks of Hormel Foods, LLC. Mark requires ® when describing meat product. Mark requires ™ when describing gaming machines.
- *State Fair*®   Registered trademark of King Show Games. Mark requires ®.
- *TABASCO*®   *TABASCO*, the *TABASCO* Bottle, and the *TABASCO* Diamond Logo are the property of McIlhenny Company, Avery Island, LA 70513, and are registered trademarks for sauces and a variety of goods and services in various jurisdictions.
- *The Three Stooges*®   © 2003 C3 Entertainment, Inc. All rights reserved. *The Three Stooges*® characters, names, and all related indicia are trademarks of C3 Entertainment, Inc. Logo requires ®.
- *The Twilight Zone*®   Registered trademark of CBS Broadcasting Inc. Mark requires ®.
- *UNO*®   © 2002 Mattel, Inc. All rights reserved. Uno is a registered trademark owned by Mattel, Inc. Mark requires ®.

- *WBA®*   Registered trademark of Japan Cash Machine Co. Ltd. and JCM American Corporation.
- *Wheel of Fortune®*   Registered trademark of Califon Productions, Inc. *Wheel of Fortune* © 2002, 2003 Califon Productions, Inc. All rights reserved. Mark requires ®. *Wheel of Fortune® Special Edition*™ *Wheel of Fortune* is a registered trademark of, and *Wheel of Fortune Special Edition* is a trademark of Califon Productions, Inc. *Wheel of Fortune* © 2002 Califon Productions, Inc. All Rights Reserved., Logo: Wheel of Fortune® Special Edition™.

Acknowledgments

First and foremost, I wish to thank my dear mother, Georgina S. Royer, for her lifetime of help, guidance, and assistance. She is a remarkable lady who fully deserves notice for her tremendous abilities and her steadfast faith in me.

I also wish to thank my literary agents, Greg Dinkin and Frank Scatoni. Greg is an accomplished author in his own right, and Frank is a widely respected book editor. Through their agency, Venture Literary, they recognized the value of what I had to offer as an author of books on casino games and gaming. Without their efforts, this book, and the others in this series, would never have come to exist.

My thanks also to Bruce Bender at Kensington Publishing, who has published this book and this series. He recognized that this book and this series offer valuable insight into the casino games as they really are, and that this book will enable almost all players to finally realize a happy and profitable casino experience. I thank Bruce, and the staff of Kensington, for their help in this process, and in particular, my editors Richard Ember and Ann LaFarge.

I extend my gratitude and thanks to my longtime friend Tom Caldwell for the many things he has done to help me and for enriching my life. I also send my thanks to Norreta, Sean, and Brent, for reasons they all know.

My sincere thanks to Bob Dempsey and his company in Las Vegas, Dempsey Graphics, for their help with many illustrations in my books. Bob, thanks also for making that videotape for me for Jay Leno and the *Tonight Show*.

To all my other friends and associates in the gaming business, from owners, managers, senior executives, hosts and supervisors: You all know who you are, and I thank you.

My friends in Australia: Neil and his family, Lilli and little MRM (Mark), Ormond College, University of Melbourne, the governor of Victoria and my former master, Sir Davis McCaughey. Also his Proctorial Eminence R. A. Dwyer, Esq. (I still have the Swiss knife you gave me more than 20 years ago), and the Alumni Association of the University of Wollongong, NSW, Department of Philosophy, and Professor Chipman. Also to the executive, editorial and display advertising staff of *The Age* newspaper in Melbourne, Australia, and to Fairfax Press in Sydney, with whom I had the pleasure of being associated at one time.

I also extend my grateful appreciation to Laurence E. Levit, C.P.A. of Los Angeles, who has been my steadfast friend, accountant, and adviser for two decades, whose faith in me and my work has never faltered. A truer friend a man rarely finds. Also to Michael Harrison, attorney-at-law in Beverly Hills, California, whose expertise and help have made my life more secure.

At this time, I wish to specifically and gratefully single out Ed Rogich from International Game Technology (IGT). I thank him for his foresight and his much appreciated assistance during the process of writing this book. Thanks to my longtime friend Rick Sorensen, also from IGT, for all his help. Mr. Rogich and Mr. Sorensen were directly instrumental in providing me with the kind of information I had to have. Without their assistance, I would not have been able to show you the photographs of those many IGT machines and games I like so much. Thanks to Cynthia White, also from IGT, for her support, as well as Connie Fox, Dawn Cox,

Robert Lightfoot, Nancy King, Todd Brown, Joe Kaminkow, Charles Cranford, and Harold Shotwell. Without the support of all these people and their valuable help and assistance, it would have been extremely difficult to tell you about the games in this book, which I have played and wanted to showcase. My thanks also to all the staff, executives, and officers of IGT, of Reno, Nevada.

Finally, to all those whose paths have crossed with mine, and who have for one reason or another stopped a while and visited. I may no longer remember your names, but I do remember what it meant to have those moments.

Thank you!

Index

About the Author

Victor H. Royer is the author of several major works on casino gambling, and is a syndicated columnist for national gaming magazines such as *Midwest Gaming and Travel* magazine, *Card Player*, *Poker Player*, and many others. He has also served as a marketing and gaming consultant to the world's largest casinos, and to gaming machine manufacturers. He lives in Las Vegas.